R A G E
AGAINST THE
MACHINE

Also by Colin Devenish

Limp Bizkit

RAGE
AGAINST THE
MACHINE

COLIN DEVENISH

 ST. MARTIN'S GRIFFIN 🐾 NEW YORK

www.stmartins.com

BOOK DESIGN BY MICHAEL COLLICA

Library of Congress Cataloging-in-Publication Data

Devenish, Colin.
    Rage Against the Machine / Colin Devenish. — 1st ed.
        p. cm.
    ISBN 0-312-27326-6
    1. Rage Against the Machine (Musical group) 2. Rock musicians — United States — Biography. I. Title.

ML421.R26 D48 2001
782.42166'092 — dc21
[B]

                                                                          2001019252

First Edition: May 2001

10 9 8 7 6 5 4 3 2 1

ACKNOWLEDGMENTS

A big shout-out to Ma, Pa, and Al, Ross, Rupal, Greg, Meg, Nod Eel, Spoon, Sharon, Nick, Morris, Giles, Liza, and anyone else who thinks they deserve it.

RAGE
AGAINST THE
MACHINE

Blending politics and music began long before any of the four members of Rage Against the Machine were born. Whether it was Woody Guthrie railing against unfair conditions in the Dust Bowl of Oklahoma during the Depression, the MC5 rallying for individual liberties, or Public Enemy offering a booming exposé of life as a black American, musicians have always found a way to lace their lyrics with subversive content. So when Rage Against the Machine burst onto the scene in the early 1990s it wasn't as though their incorporation of a pointed political agenda into their aggressive songs marked the arrival of the much-heralded horse of a different color. What set Rage apart from the typical rockers with a cause who bop in ten minutes before the charity gig, hop up onstage, yell out a few "How ya doin', Clevelands," and hop back in the tour bus, was a lasting commitment to the issues they supported.

When singer Zack de la Rocha developed an interest in

the political strife in the Chiapas region of Mexico, he volunteered to help out and spent weeks at a time working with the campesinos and learned firsthand about their situation. And over the years he has continued to return, and taken advantage of the platform Rage has to draw attention to the issue. A similar pattern has developed over the years with other human-rights cases and situations where it appears justice might have taken a backseat to political necessity. In some cases, such as that of Mumia Abu-Jamal, Rage Against the Machine's decision to play benefits on his behalf and to publicize his case ignited a great backlash against the band, with the Fraternal Order of Police, the governor of New Jersey, and the mighty Howard Stern all speaking out against the band's interest and involvement in the case.

Rage Against the Machine wasn't the first group to combine elements of hip-hop with the filthy dirge of heavy metal, but when guitarist Tom Morello realized that the shredder era had come and gone, he worked on developing a new guitar sound, one that showcased his ample chops but which also stretched to create the sounds hip-hop bands usually turned to a DJ to make. Drummer Brad Wilk and bassist Tim Commerford were hardly the first rhythm section to lock it up tight, but by keeping a rock-solid groove, they allowed Zack time for his onstage rants and provided the foundation that allowed Tom to play DJ with his endless bag of guitar tricks and still hop back into the song at the drop of a hat. Rage Against the Machine weren't the first ones to do what they do, but after three platinum-plus–selling albums, multiple world tours, and, later, countless kids having woken up to the possibilities of political action, it would be tough for the judges of the compulsories to look at their overall performance and not give them a ten.

But bands don't spring from the womb fully formed. Before Rage was a provocative, united force of music and politics they were four guys growing up in decidedly different environments, who each chose music as an outlet for their creative energies and frustrations and as a means toward creating something more than they'd been given.

When Zack de la Rocha was a year old, his parents split and he grew up switching off between his mother's home in Irvine, California, and his father's Lincoln Heights neighborhood in Los Angeles. Beto de la Rocha, Zack's father, was part of the Chicano art collective Los Four, along with Carlos Alamaz, Frank Romero, and Gilbert Lujan, which in 1974 was the first group of Mexican-American artists to have an exhibit displayed at the Los Angeles County Museum of Art.

"They were artists who realized that art as a medium is also very political by nature," Zack told *Raygun* magazine. "[Beto] would do a series of paintings for the United Farm Workers depicting, like, Mexican history to make it visible to the public. He and the other members, Carlos Alamaz,

Frank Romero, and Gilbert Lujan, all tried to document that and make it accessible to the community, and I think that's what we're trying to do with music."

At an age when most kids' minds are cluttered with nothing more pressing than Little League baseball or gabbing on the phone, a young Zack de la Rocha got his first taste of a decidedly bitter American tradition. As Zack sat in class listening to what ostensibly was supposed to be a lecture on the geological makeup of California's coast, his teacher made an off-the-cuff remark that accidentally sparked a revolution in Zack's mind.

"He was describing one of the areas between San Diego and Oceanside, and as a reference to this particular area of the coastline, he said, 'You know, that wetback station there.' And everyone around me laughed," recalled Zack in *Rolling Stone*. "They thought it was the funniest thing that they ever heard. I remember sitting there, about to explode. I realized that I was not of these people. They were not my friends. And I remember internalizing it, how silent I was. I remember how afraid I was to say anything."

The lone Mexican-American in a classroom in Irvine, California—a conservative city in California's ultraconservative Orange County—the teacher's offhand crack caused Zack to see for the first time how casual and accepted racism can be. With his mother completing her Ph.D. in anthropology at the University of California at Irvine, packing up and moving out was not an option. Instead of altering his physical location, young Zack vowed to abandon his stunned silence and speak out. "I told myself that I would never allow myself to not respond to that type of situation—in any form, anywhere," Zack told *Rolling Stone*.

Living in Irvine meant Zack needed to learn a way to voice his discontent with the status quo while in the midst of people determined to keep things as is. "The rule for Chicanos was you were there because you had a mop or a broom in your hand or a hammer, or filled baskets of strawberries. Those things started a process for me which was intensely introspective and questioning of everything around me. . . . I feel kind of somewhere in between those worlds. There's this duality, because I'm constantly having to juggle between those two cultural experiences."

Zack knew he was capable of a lot more than what the stereotypes he experienced in Irvine would have him be. From an early age he turned to music as an outlet to help him express himself and the person he was becoming. In an interview CD chronicling Rage's career, Zack talked about his early influences. "I started playing guitar when I was eight and I played mostly punk at first, but then in junior high a music teacher turned me on to Joe Pass and Charlie Parker. At the time I was in a punk band called Juvenile Expression, and jazz opened me up to the possibilities of improvisations and hybrids."

Current bandmate and longtime pal Tim Commerford also was a member of Juvenile Expression, and offered his impressions of a young Zack in the pages of *Spin*. "We played a lot of basketball, even though he was real small; we skateboarded all over. When I first met him at his house, he had this acoustic guitar, and he eventually taught me how to play the entire Sex Pistols album. We were in a band in seventh grade called Juvenile Expression. He was breakin' at school when nobody else knew what hip-hop was. That kid was on it from day one."

In the early 1980s hip-hop still seemed like a renegade form of music, with rock hard-liners insisting it was just a bass-happy fad that would disappear in the same sudden way disco had died. In case you missed the last twenty years of music history—they were wrong. Rap records routinely take over the top slot of the weekly *Billboard* Top 200 charts. Ninety-five-year-old grandmothers have heard Sisqó's "Thong Song," and even your geeky older brother has a Dr. Dre album around somewhere.

Up until the late eighties, bands were either straight-up hip-hop or rock, with little middle ground. The idea that they could blend together was a little like saying red could be blue, up just might be down, and the difference between being dead or alive is slight. The barriers tumbled slowly, beginning with Run-D.M.C.'s collaboration with Aerosmith, which introduced rap to fans who would never have dreamed of listening to anything but classic rock and presented classic rock in a new context that turned heads in the hip-hop world. Anthrax's pairing with band heroes Public Enemy on the P.E. track "Bring the Noise" would provide the closest thing to a template for what Rage would later do.

In southern California, where Zack was growing up, the battle lines were clearly drawn. You liked rock or hip-hop and never the two shall meet. Zack's punk pals clapped their hands over their ears at the mention of phat beats and fresh cuts and breaks, but Zack heard more than tight rhymes and booming bass in the fledgling art form.

"I was listening to hip-hop early on, growing up in both East Los Angeles and Orange County, and I had a lot of white friends who refused to talk to me the second I put on an Adidas sweatsuit and was breaking, or I was walking through campus with my radio playing Eric B. and Rakim, and LL Cool J and De La Soul," Zack told *Rolling Stone*. "To so many whites it was just noise. To me, it was people reclaiming their dignity."

More than any other band member, the political good that Rage has been able to achieve was Zack's primary motivation to write songs, make records, and tour. In an interview with *Rolling Stone*, he went one better and said it was the only reason he was in Rage. For an accomplished musician to take such a stance is pretty serious stuff, but to see where Zack gets this intense idealism one need look no farther than his father Beto, a talented painter who for a while chose not to sell his work, even when the de la Rocha family didn't have money to buy food. "He was a very interesting character," Zack said to *Rolling Stone*. "He

COLIN DEVENISH

refused to sell his artwork. 'What do you mean, sell my pieces? This is popular art.' I admire him for his position. But his sense of realism, given the situation — 'Look, there are only so many roaches we're gonna pull out of the cereal box.'"

Beto suffered a severe nervous breakdown in 1981. Zack's home life in Irvine was uncomfortable, and he felt isolated because of his race, but after Beto's breakdown, his Lincoln Heights home became an uneasy one as well. No longer believing in his work, Beto invested his energies in a rigid and obsessive religious faith and, when Zack came to visit on weekends, imposed his new philosophies on his son. "I would go to see him on weekends down in Lincoln Heights and be forced to sit in a room with the curtains drawn and the door locked," Zack said in *Raygun*. "He forced me to fast. I went through some really intense stuff."

Beto quit his job at East Los Angeles Community College and spent his days indoors, reading the Bible incessantly and ultimately taking the biblical commandment to not make graven images so seriously that he wrecked much of his own artwork, and forced Zack to destroy it as well. Zack described that time in an interview with *Spin* magazine. "He burned over 60 percent of his artwork. It was very, very, very difficult and at one point he forced me to burn it for him. These were paintings that I grew up around and loved and admired him for creating. I had no clue why he'd want me to destroy them."

In an interview with the *Los Angeles Times*, Beto partially attributed his downward spiral to his frustration at being unable to make a living in art on his own terms. "With the museum thing, I expected the whole world to open up to me. [But] nothing happened. I didn't know how to wait for success, how to be patient. I had this idea back then that once you began to work as an artist you could buy your car and have food to eat and raise your family. That doesn't happen. Very few people make any money at this profession."

With his two homes less than happy, Zack found refuge in music and a close-knit core group of friends who shared his passion for punk rock. As he listened to his favorite punk bands, he heard something besides lightning-quick guitars and furious ranting. While many kids get caught up in the fashion of punk or revel in the opportunity to mosh in a pit, Zack discovered something else. Reading between the lines, he taught himself the do-it-yourself work ethic that made it possible for small punk bands to make records and tour on a modest budget. One of punk's lasting legacies will always be that after the Sex Pistols' self-professed amateurish assault on the rock world, little things like talent were suddenly not so important. With minimal equipment and skill and a healthy combination of anger, guts, and the belief that "Loud Fast Rules!" punk was there for the taking. Zack caught on to this concept quickly and soon realized the only difference between himself and his heroes were a mic and a stage to use it on. "Whenever I used to listen to bands like Government Issue, Minor Threat, or Scream, it always made me feel like I would just lose it if I had a microphone in my hand," Zack told *Alternative Press* Magazine. "It's such a healthy thing to get onstage and vent—especially in the hardcore scene. Anyone can just get up there and express themselves. Anyone."

That "anyone" became *someone* with the band Inside Out. Brothers Mark and Rob Hayworth were part of Zack's early ensemble Hard Stance, which later evolved into Inside Out. In an interview with *Spin*, Rob "Cubby" Hayworth said that growing up different in Irvine provided major inspiration for their music. "That place was so fucked that you'd feel bad for not driving a Jaguar to school. We decided to play punk music to rebel against where we were. Every house looked the same; cops were everywhere, pulling you over for the way you dressed or the color of your skin. Zack dealt with racial shit all the time."

If there were an advantage to Zack growing up in Irvine, it was only that his miserable experience growing up there gave him ample experience in questioning authority. Loath to accept the status quo, he developed an increasingly independent streak to his thinking and assumed responsibility for his own education after he left high school. "I think my high-school experience pushed me through a crisis of identity, it enabled me to be more of a critical individual," he told *Vox*. "It made me question the institution I was forced to adjust to and my relationship with society. Those four

years or so during high school were what eventually polit-
icized me, 'cause the experience made me step and back
and take a look at how I was being indoctrinated. Once
I'd left, I became engaged in reading and since then, I've
gone through my own self-education."

Instead of walking around breaking stuff, as some bands
might suggest, Zack diverted his fury into his music, combining his outrage with a growing awareness of how the
world works, evolving into the sort of lyrics he would eventually become famous for. In an interview CD chronicling
Rage's career, Zack talked about the factors that led to his
strident lyrical approach. "My political awakening came in
high school when I realized you're really only successful
in this country when you've been completely assimilated
and you've achieved a lot materially. So the oppression that
ordinary people are constantly subjected to is as much spiritual as political. If our music sounds angry, it's because
we're fighting for empowerment on a spiritual level as well
as a material one. When I sing a song it's a reflection of
my inner self as well as my social philosophy."

Inside Out landed a key gig when they hopped on a tour
with Quicksand and Shelter, both of which featured former
members of the hardcore act Youth of Today. Eager for
the chance to bring their music and message to kids across
the country, Inside Out scrambled to make the tour happen. Zack's courage quickly got put to the test three thousand miles from home at a June 15, 1990, gig at the

Anthrax club in Norwalk, Connecticut, when punks in attendance circulated fliers with Nazi symbols on them, protesting Shelter's ties to the Hare Krishna movement.

Zack didn't hesitate. "If anyone thinks this swastika belongs on the same piece of paper as this Krishna symbol, you're all just fucking ignorant," he said, and then ripped up the offending flier. Mike Rosas now plays guitar in Smile but he once played alongside Zack in Inside Out. In an interview with the *Orange County Weekly*, Rosas said Zack always made it a priority to get his point across to fans. "I guess it's kind of the same thing now, but he had a lot of great things to say. When we would play shows, he would take a lot of time to explain what the songs were about and really try to get the message across. I think a lot of times, it was a big challenge because people just wanted to slam-dance. But at the same time, it made a difference — a lot of people paid attention to him and went on to start other bands. A lot of bands you see nowadays are definitely influenced by Inside Out and other bands that existed in the early nineties."

Inside Out gave Zack a chance to learn the frontman trade, and the title of an album they would never release gave Rage Against the Machine its name. Inside Out released their only EP, *Spiritual Surrender*, on Revelation Records, an indie label based in Huntington Beach, California. Jordan Cooper, owner of Revelation, offered his recollections of a young Zack and early Inside Out in an interview with the *Orange County Weekly*. "Inside Out were pretty popular in O.C. back in 1990 and '91. They were great, one of the best bands of that time period. And Zack was one of the funniest people I've ever met. I was really surprised that he got into politics and activism. He always seemed to be more into making people laugh."

Tom Morello's mother, Mary, was teaching on a military base in Kenya when she met Ngethe Njoroge, a Mau Mau revolutionary who would later become Tom's father. They were married in 1963, after Kenya had won its independence from Great Britain and his father was selected to be part of a Kenyan delegation to the U.N. in New York. They lived in New York for about a year after Tom was born, until his parents divorced and his father returned to Kenya and, ironically enough, became one of the wealthier landowners in that country. Tom's uncle was Mzee Jomo Kenyatta, who had returned to Kenya after a seven-year exile in the 1950s and served as the first Kenyan president until his death in 1978.

After his parents' split, Mary and Tom moved back to her native Illinois in 1964. Returning to Illinois with her son proved to be an eye-opening experience, as Mary quickly learned that middle America wasn't up to accepting a white mother and her black son. The two found housing tough to find and attitudes impossible to change. Tom explained the circumstances that led to their settling in the Chicago suburb of Libertyville in an interview with the *Chicago Tribune*. "When she was originally looking for a teaching job in the north suburban area, Libertyville was the first that would allow her to teach in the public school system and us to live in the community. . . . All the other communities said, 'Well, you can teach here, but you and your little brown-skinned boy are going to have to live somewhere else.' People were talking about property values when a little one-year-old Kenyan kid was trying to move into the neighborhood."

Single-handedly integrating the predominantly white suburb meant that a young Tom Morello first encountered racism before he could fully grasp the concept. Six-year-old Tom found himself repeatedly being called "nigger" by the daughter of the woman that ran his daycare. Uncertain of the meaning but sure it was bad, it was only when he sobbingly sought an explanation from his mother that he fully understood the slur. In addition to comforting Tom, Mary Morello gave him the lowdown on Malcolm X and other black leaders who encouraged firm and sometimes militant resistance to racist behavior. The next day after daycare, Tom came home telling a whole new story. "The girl started calling me names again on the next day, but this time, I fired off with 'Shut up, whitey!' and I clocked her with my little fist," Tom told *Alternative Press*. "It created enough of a commotion so that the daycare woman came over and scrubbed her daughter's mouth out." Seeing this kind of ingrained racism at that age caused Tom to become acutely conscious of his color and the impact it had on some of his not-so-worldly neighbors.

Knowing the challenges Tom faced growing up in Libertyville, Mary Morello set about teaching him about the
causes of racism and explaining some of the core factors that
affect race relations in America, and built a solid foundation
for him to understand the larger picture he was a small part
of in Libertyville. In an interview with the *Chicago Tribune*,
Tom talked about the crash course in sociology his mom
gave him to help him cope with and understand his situation. "My mother laid the groundwork; she prepared me in
a unique way to deal with what goes on in America, to face
what it meant to be African-American in a white society. By
the time I got to high school, I knew enough to be completely disgusted with what was being taught in history class.
I was not exactly in sync with the thinking that Columbus
was this benign explorer, because I had come to view him as
this genocidal conqueror."

Years later Tom told the *Chicago Tribune* he has mixed
feelings about the place where he spent the first eighteen
years of his life. Although he made good friends there,
some of the experiences he had growing up made an in-
delible mark. "I don't have any regrets about growing up
there because it was a beautiful, peaceful place to live
where I made friends who will be friends for the rest of
my life, including Adam and Maureen from Tool and
Babes in Toyland. But there was always an element of racism. One morning I woke up and there was a noose hang-
ing in the garage. There were some incidents. Something
that not a lot of kids have to go through."

Tom started playing guitar at the relatively old age of seventeen. He'd first picked up a guitar four years earlier but quit the lessons in frustration when his teacher started him off tuning his guitar and playing scales instead of teaching Tom the huge KISS and Led Zeppelin riffs he wanted to play. "I gave this guy five dollars and told him that's what I wanted to learn," Tom told *Jersey Rocks*. "But he said, 'No, little Tommy—first we have to learn to tune the guitar.' I thought that was a huge waste of time when there were so many cool songs to be learned. But I tuned the guitar, and when I went back the next week he said, 'Now we have to learn how to play a C-major scale.' That was it—no more guitar lessons for me." Tom's hiatus from guitar ended when he heard the Sex Pistols' amateurish thrashing on record and realized you can be in a band without being a guitar god, or even having any discernible talent. Soon Tom was stumbling through the basic chords on his guitar, with classmate and future Tool guitarist Adam Jones strumming alongside him in the unforgettable yet short-lived punk band Electric Sheep, which took its name from a passage of a sci-fi book titled *Do Androids Dream of Electric Sheep?* by Philip K. Dick. (The 1982 film *Blade Runner*, directed by Ridley Scott and starring Harrison Ford, is also based on this book.)

Playing with Electric Sheep got Tom started in songwriting, and he became familiar with the ins and outs of band dynamics, but his unusual taste meant he made no progress in the area that means most to high-school guitar heroes. "I couldn't play many songs in high school. Just my own. There were guys who could play anything by anybody, but couldn't write to save their life," Tom recalled in *Guitar One*. "But in high school, it was a mark of shame if you couldn't cover the Doobie Brothers. You weren't getting chicks. Period. Okay? Here we were a weird punk rock band with Devo influences—not high on the food chain. The ladies were having none of it."

Tom's tastes in music might have kept him from being a lady-killer, but his interest in *Star Trek, Dungeons and Dragons*, and Karl Marx probably didn't help. Concerned that he had some catching-up to do, he began an intense practice regimen that began at an hour each day and swelled to a borderline manic eight hours a day while in college at Harvard. "It was to the point where it was really obsessive," Tom recounted to *Guitar One*. "I would not play one hour and fifty-six minutes a day, I would play two hours a day. Come hell or high water, if I had a 103-degree fever, I would play two hours a day. If I had a big exam the next morning, and it was two o'clock in the morning, I would play until four in the morning, without exception."

Even though Tom started thrashing his way through "Anarchy in the U.K." and "Rock and Roll All Nite" well after his pimply peers had, he never doubted that his hours of militant practice would one day be the sole source of his income. By the age of nineteen, a full two years after he had started playing guitar, he vowed he would one day make his living playing rock. "Did you ever see *The Decline of Western Civilization Part Two: The Metal Years*? I felt like one of those kids who said, 'This is what I'm going to do if it kills me.' There's that excellent montage where the interviewer asks, 'What if you don't make it?' And the answer was, 'Well, that's not an option.' She says, 'What's your Plan B?' And the answer is, 'There is no Plan B.' I had no Plan B," Tom told *Guitar One*.

After a year at Harvard, Tom came home for the summer and tried out for some bands in the Chicago area, played with a Renaissance fair, and considered junking the Harvard experience for playing other people's songs on the wedding, bar mitzvah, and backyard-BBQ circuit. In retrospect Tom explained his reasoning for staying in school instead of joining the cover band of his dreams to guitar.com: "At the time they seemed like the Rolling Stones even though they were really just crummy cover bands. I was able to play in bars I was too young to drink in and I could have chosen to stay there and keep playing but I thought, 'I got into Harvard. I ought to finish what I started.'"

When not holed up in his room completing his intense guitar-practice regimen, Tom kept his finger on the political pulse at Harvard, demonstrating in favor of divestment from South Africa during the waning days of apartheid and writing his senior thesis on the student uprisings going on in that country.

During a trip to Europe, omnipresent guitar in tow, Tom happened into a record shop playing a rap album. Just as hearing the Sex Pistols' *Never Mind the Bollocks* had made him dust off his disused guitar and join a band, hearing hip-hop for the first time got him listening to a style of music that would go on to heavily influence his playing. "I heard a record by Grandmaster Flash and the Furious Five in a record shop," Tom told *Guitar One*. "It was the first time I had heard rap music. It was called 'Revival' and I immediately bought the 12-inch. That literally changed my life, and broke me out of the mold of white suburban rock. Until then, it had all been either punk rock or hard rock. I didn't really know that other kinds of music existed. Sure my mom had James Brown and Stevie Wonder records around the house, but I thought, 'Man, those don't really have kickin' guitar solos. That can't be music.' "

As a kid reading magazines about his heavy-metal heroes, Tom thought Los Angeles seemed like the place where rock was made, and even after four years at Harvard the idea of playing guitar, even in some of Hollywood's seediest clubs, was appealing enough to convince Tom to move to L.A. The dream for the last fifty years hasn't changed much. It shapes up something like this. Kid in [fill in the blank: suburban Midwestern, Southern . . . what-have-you . . .] town plays a musical instrument and daydreams about going to L.A. and getting signed. Kid comes of age and decides to throw all his eggs in that shaky

basket and head west come hell or high water. Kid eats
Top Ramen, sleeps on floors and does session work for
years, gets fat and bitter. Or, kid hits it big, fulfills the
dream, spends a decade surrounded by hookers and blow
and comes home a hero. In either scenario it always happens in Los Angeles, with its countless clubs and the clout
of nearby record companies fueling the dream. So while
his college roommates started on their respective paths toward careers in medicine, investment banking, and as a
college professor, Tom arrived in Los Angeles in 1986 with
a Harvard degree and too many qualifications to get him
a job. In an interview with *Jersey Rocks* Tom explained his
choice to go west. "From reading hard-rock magazines, I
understood that Los Angeles was the place you had to go.
So I moved there with no roots, no friends, just a list of
names from the Harvard Alumni Association! I expected
that I would find a big pool of great musicians, and I could
find someone with whom I could meld my interest in politics. Nothing could have been further from the truth—I
got there at the height of the glam era when Poison and
Faster Pussycat were on top."

Not wanting to become a corporate guy, but very much
wanting to make enough to eat and put a roof over his
head, Tom found himself wading in a shockingly shallow
job pool for someone of his educational background. "I
did telemarketing, and mind-numbing temp work. For
months, my job was alphabetizing and filing," he said in
Guitar World. "Basically I was treated like a dog. . . . Inse-

✪ 2 0 ✪

curity in such good business. When you have to call up every morning at seven to find out if you have a job or not, there's no way you're going to be organizing a union or trying to get a higher wage."

Arriving during the heyday of glam metal, finding musicians who shared the breadth of his musical interests was a daunting task. Tom placed an ad in the *L.A. Weekly* that read, "Wanted: Socialist lead singer for Public Enemy–style metal band." Tom got some nibbles but in an interview with the *Sacramento Bee*, he said that most of the responses ran pretty far afield. "No one wanted to play with me. I had an idea that mixed elements of Run-D.M.C. and Black Sabbath with a political context, but the closest thing I found was one guy who liked both Janet Jackson and Poison."

In the early stages of Tom's rock odyssey he enjoyed the support of an unlikely ally, his mom. Mary Morello's career in activism had included work with the NAACP and the Urban League in the 1960s and 1970s, and in the 1980s she turned her keen political eye to rock, founding Parents for Rock and Rap as a counter to the pro-censorship groups popular at that time. Her militant anti-censorship stance led her to crusade for First Amendment rights for 2 Live Crew, and in her quest for tolerance she took on political heavyweights such as former Kansas senator and presidential candidate Bob Dole. In an interview with the *Chicago Tribune*, Mary Morello discussed the factors that led to her becoming so intensely involved with the free-speech cause.

"Censorship is coming down now harder than it has before. Look at the Congress that we have—trying to take funds away from the National Endowment for the Arts, trying to kill public television. They must be living in the Dark Ages."

Before Rage formed, Tom played guitar in Lock-Up. They released a record on a major label and were dropped in the blink of an eye, and almost as quickly as he thought he'd made it, he was back to square one. In an interview with the *Los Angeles Times* Tom talked about his short-lived tenure with Lock-Up. "We had a two-album guaranteed deal. But when our first record flopped, the label dropped the band. We asked about the second record and they said in effect, 'Do you have the money to sue us?' And of course we didn't."

After Lock-Up broke up, Tom sought a means of enacting change by working within the system. This meant a job working as the scheduling secretary for longtime California senator Alan Cranston. Well-known for his liberal agenda, Cranston seemed like the kind of politician that might understand and share the concerns Tom had. In the end, though, Tom's time with Cranston taught him a painful lesson about the behind-the-scene machinations that dominate politics.

"Cranston was probably as far left of a senator as you're going to get, but it didn't really matter. Despite the fact that he had progressive views on the environment or immigration, he spent all day on the phone calling the wealthy and powerful, exchanging favors for campaign money. I realized that once he was elected, who would he owe? Would he owe single mothers, the homeless, and the guy working at Kentucky Fried Chicken, or would he owe ITT, GE, and other savings-and-loan tycoons?"

Even apart from the canvassing of fat cats, Tom himself felt confined by political protocol. Once, a woman called up demanding Cranston do something about the influx of Mexicans into her neighborhood; Tom put her in her place, only to take heat from Cranston staffers for not taking a more delicate approach. "I had a woman ring up incensed because there were Mexicans moving into her neighborhood," Tom recounted to *Kerrang!* "I told her that it's far better to be living in a neighborhood of Mexicans than a neighborhood of loudmouth racists. I thought I was doing good work but I was chewed out by all of my employers for my honesty."

Brad Wilk's love affair with the drums began before he ever smacked the skins, when a neighbor's kit caught his eye. "When I was about thirteen years old, in Chicago, a friend of mine who lived a couple doors down had a Ludwig Silver Sparkle drum kit with a big KISS logo on the front head," Brad recollected in *Drum!* "I was totally infatuated with the drum set—period. So any time I could, I was on his kit, not knowing what the hell I was doing but banging away nonetheless."

His parents bought him a guitar and Brad spent a couple

years trying to ape Eddie Van Halen but his true musical epiphany came during Little League when Steve Miller Band's "Fly Like an Eagle" came on over the public-address system. As he stood in taking his hacks, he heard something much more than classic rock at a T-ball game. "I remember being in a batting cage during Little League and hearing the song over the PA," Brad said in an interview with *Modern Drummer.* "That was the moment I understood instrumentation and where it was coming from. It was no longer foreign to me. I could pick things out and understand what was happening musically."

After that life-changing experience of hearing "Fly Like an Eagle" Brad began paying closer attention to music and the drums in particular. The 1979 release of the Who's retrospective double album, *The Kids Are Alright* (soundtrack to the Who film of the same title), gave Brad his first exposure to the volatile drumming style of Keith Moon. Although the drummer had died of a drug overdose a year earlier, the controlled chaos in Moon's playing captivated Brad and inspired him to take lessons. "I love the fact that Keith Moon played with this unbelievable confidence, but he was on the edge of insanity. He was a driving force, but he was always just on the brink of completely losing his mind."

Determined to give his high-school band a venue to play their Zeppelin covers in relative peace, Brad turned thief to make his rock dreams a reality. "In high school I played with friends in garage bands while working in a store that sold comforters. I remember stealing thirty comforters to soundproof our garage," Brad confessed to *Modern Drummer*. "I'm not proud of stealing, but I'd do anything at that point to play."

Lessons from David Garibaldi and close study of jazz drummer Elvin Jones added a jazzy, funked-up flavor to Brad's drumming, which he fused with his love of Keith Moon's edgy playing, cultivating his own style. In an interview with *Drum!* Brad credited Garibaldi with getting him to better understand the drummer's role in a band. "[Garibaldi] really taught me to focus on what's going on between the beats. The stuff that's kind of felt, less heard . . . That all goes back to James Brown and George Clinton. If you listen to P-Funk, a song like 'Downstroke,' and listen to just how heavy and slightly late he's coming down on that 'one.' He's waiting for everybody, so everyone's going to get it and know where they [are]."

After high school Brad worked odd jobs to keep himself afloat and to pay for his drum equipment. In an interview with *Modern Drummer* Brad said his ferocious playing caused him to spend an inordinate amount of his meager wages on replacing cymbals. "I delivered pizzas at my friend's pizza place. I did what I had to to make ends meet. Delivering pizzas let me drive around and listen to loud music. That job enabled me to buy cymbals, which were cracking left and right. I used to drill holes in the cymbals to stop the cracks."

As a kid, Brad bounced around, living in Portland and

Chicago, logging his high-school years at Taft High School in Los Angeles, the very same school rapper and fellow famous guy Ice Cube attended. Much of the instability in his home life stemmed from his father's obsession with money and the many professions—from bookie to jeweler—he tried his hand at in attempts to get more of it. In an interview with *Raygun*, Brad talked about how his father's intense materialism impacted him in the opposite way. "I'm trying to live my life and find happiness in pretty basic things and not put a whole lot of emphasis on money either. That was everything to my father, and I saw it kind of ruin him. It made me really try and appreciate the things that don't cost money, which are the things that should be appreciated anyway."

Moving around as often as an army brat taught Brad to appreciate situations for what they are, a quality that would lead to him becoming the diplomat in Rage, the member best able to put his ego on the shelf when a consensus needed to be established. His willingness to be flexible probably went a long way toward keeping Rage together during the tougher times, but in an interview with *Raygun* he explained that he wished he wasn't always so eager to increase the peace. "I think I have too much empathy. Tom believes that as well about me. I find myself stuck in between situations, and instead of coming to a decision based on what I feel, I'm always looking at everyone else's feelings, and how it's going to affect every person. It just makes things really difficult. I really wish I could just be a fucking asshole sometimes."

The youngest of five kids, Tim Commerford's life changed radically at age seven when his mom was diagnosed with brain cancer. Once a talented mathematician, her condition degenerated so rapidly that by the time he was in third grade she was unable to help him with his math homework. She lived until Tim was twenty but her illness put an incredible strain on the family. His father, an aeronautics/space engineer who worked on the space shuttle, eventually left his mother and remarried. Tim got bounced around and spent some time living with his sister in Sacramento. "I had no traditional upbringing of any sort. Rage has been my upbringing. Zack is one of the few people still in my life who knew my mom and who can talk to me about that time." With his home life in turmoil, Tim found stability in playing his bass. On an interview CD detailing the history of the band, Tim talked about what helped keep him sane as a kid. "I was really into being a hermit. I spent a lot of time in my bedroom when I was a kid just learning how to play bass, playing along with records."

His senior year, Tim said sayonara to his role as a defensive end on the high-school football team and devoted his full focus to learning Rush covers and his burgeoning career as a gas-station attendant. "I was totally hung up on that *Moving Pictures* album," Tim told *Spin*. "I ended up working at Campus Gas, paying rent to my dad." His prospects at that point looked bleak, but within a few years his dim future, and that of his future bandmates, would brighten considerably.

After finding each other through classified ads, Rage crammed into a room and started jamming to see if they'd made a match. Tom recalled his first meeting with Zack in an interview in *Jersey Rocks*. "It was at this tiny, cramped rehearsal space with a PA system you could hardly hear. Zack came with a couple of his friends, and started rapping. But because of this horrible PA, I had no idea of what the lyrical content was, and there wasn't enough room for him to express himself in the way he does on-stage."

The early rehearsals were electric. After years of searching for an elusive sound with earlier outfits, all four members of Rage knew in the early days of practice at the grimy rehearsal space out in the Valley that the hunt was over. In an interview with the Australian magazine *The Age*, Brad talked about those early jam sessions with the guys who responded to his ad, that read "drummer looking for a band with many different influences to form own unique sound." "Unbelievably enough, the chemistry was undeniable and intact, and I remember being blown away from day one. All of us realized, 'Holy shit, there's something going on here that we need to explore,' and it just snowballed from there. It is definitely a collaboration. I may come in with a bit, or Tom will come in with a riff, or Tim will come in with a bass line, and it grows from there. No one ever comes in with a song and says, 'Hear this,' which I think is one of the best parts about being in this band. . . ."

Straight out of the gate, Rage Against the Machine emphasized the political component of the group, beginning with the name of the band. Originally slated as an album title for Zack's former outfit, Inside Out, de la Rocha liked the name and its significance well enough to suggest it to the new members of what became Rage Against the Machine. "I wanted to think of something metaphorical that described my frustrations living in a political and economic system which fuels itself off the blood of oppressed people all over the world for the last five centuries," Zack told *Rip* magazine. "A machine doesn't have any humane understanding. To me, it was the perfect metaphor to describe the structure of the establishment."

With a name and some songs in progress, Rage were anxious to see if the chemistry they all felt in the practice room would translate to the stage. Needing somewhere to put it to the test, they put the word out and then waited.

Like many bands before them, Rage got their first gig from the "I got this friend" network, meaning somebody they knew, knew somebody was having a party, and after some phone calls and some worrying about the cops, Rage got the go-ahead to play at a friend's of Tim's house. Five and a half songs later and they were veterans of the hard-to-crack, Huntington Beach living-room circuit, and eager to branch out and find new living rooms to play and maybe even clubs. The partiers' enthusiastic response meant that the count of living-room gigs would stay at one, and soon L.A.'s rock venues were getting a taste of what the lucky horde that packed into some guy's living room in Huntington Beach had seen first.

Brad recalled the band's first club gig in an interview with *Kerrang!* "The first show we played was at a club called Jabberjaw in L.A. in 1991. We rehearsed for two or three months and decided to fuck the record companies and just sell the tape ourselves at the show. The crowd reaction was so intense that it was a big celebration of frustration and anger. It was a remarkable feeling. I realized that we had something special and that maybe we could take this thing further."

Tom remembers the early shows in a similar way: wowed audiences growing exponentially with each gig. The word-of-mouth network functioned more seamlessly than PR, and at a time when most bands are papering flyers on telephone polls and bribing their friends to come to the show with false promises of free drinks, Rage was playing to increasingly full houses. "During our first couple of club shows we amassed a rabid following. It was amazing how quickly people learned the words to the songs. One guy from each show was obviously telling twenty more guys about us, based on how the shows grew from the start."

Getting those early gigs was made easier by the fact that Adam Jones, Tom's old buddy from high school, was playing guitar in Tool, the "buzz band" of the moment on the L.A. scene. Instead of playing soul-killing gigs in front of the bartender, a couple toothless drunks, and that rube who's always gotta yell out for "Skynyrd!" Rage were soon playing to packed clubs. "We were fortunate, because my old friend Adam Jones was in the big local band at the time—Tool!" Tom told *Jersey Rocks*. "We got to open shows for them and play for full houses, and we got a major-label offer after our second show."

Rage got their start as a shift in the L.A. music scene was getting under way. The hair-metal gods that had strutted up and down the Sunset Strip throughout the 1980s were starting to get the dinosaur treatment and began considering haircuts and adding non-leather pants to their wardrobes. The walking-tour-of-the-fretboard guitar solos popularized by Eddie Van Halen were starting to fall from favor. Some guitarists, in desperation, were even reverting back to writing songs. Seeing a couple virtuosos wanking at an early gig caused Tom to take his guitar-playing in a different direction. ". . . The guitarist in this first band was just absolutely shredding—just liquid fingers playing Eric

Johnson solos note for note. Then the next band comes on and they have two guitarists doing the same thing. Then I thought to myself, 'If there are three guys in two cover bands on one stage doing this, there certainly doesn't need to be a fourth,' " he laughingly recalled to *Guitar School*. "And while their playing was certainly accomplished, it really dawned on me that any kind of originality was going to have to come from somewhere else."

Being in a band like Rage, which blended hip-hop and rock, meant that a unique style of guitar-playing was required. Simply strumming a tune or showcasing his solo chops wouldn't cut the mustard so Tom worked at adapting his play to fit the new genre that was developing. "I was really excited about the prospect of playing hip-hop music within the context of a punk-rock band, and I wasn't going to make any excuses for there not being a DJ!" Tom explained to *Guitar World*. "At that time, my chief influences were Terminator X and Jam Master Jay, and I was determined to re-create the record-scratching, DJ stuff—those rich, bizarre textures—on my guitar." As testimony to his hard work, Rage's first record came with an advisory in the liner notes that read, "No samples, keyboards or synthesizers used in the making of this recording," which simply meant all the unworldly squeaks and squawks on the album were coaxed from the strings and surface of Tom's helplessly compliant electric guitar. Interestingly, Tom's first foray into noise experimentation came as a teenager, when he was charged with scoring his friends' homemade horror films. "When I was nineteen, some of my friends were aspiring filmmakers. One day we just said, 'Let's make a movie today.' So we did a trilogy of horror films and I did the soundtracks. . . . That experience really pushed me into creating sounds. It also made me learn how to get the most out of my little four-track. That was a formative experience."

Zack's intensity is now the stuff of legend, as anyone who's seen his eyes bulging and heard his furious shrieks on albums and onstage can attest, but in the early days it was new even to his bandmates. Tom recalled in an interview with *Addicted to Noise* that Zack's rebel yell hit top volume in early rehearsals at their San Fernando Valley practice space and then during the actual writing of the songs. "I remember there was a fateful day where I think we were writing the song 'Township Rebellion' and up to that point, Zack had just been rapping. . . . He did this just terrifyingly beautiful yell. It hit me in the same way as the Who's—what's that song—'Won't Be Fooled Again,' where he does that thing, where you go, 'Oh my gosh, it just couldn't be better.' "

All that fury has to come from somewhere, and in the interview CD documenting the history of the band, Zack traced the origins of his anger to the days when he was a teenager, before he had status and before he had a pager. At this time he had recognized the influence capitalism had on himself and oppressed peoples everywhere. To say this realization didn't sit well is an understatement on the level of saying that during World War Two, a couple people died. "My political awakening came in high school when I realized you're really only successful in this country when you've been completely assimilated and you've achieved a lot materially. So the oppression that ordinary people are constantly subjected to is as much spiritual as political. If our music sounds angry, it's because we're fighting for empowerment on a spiritual level as well as a material one. When I sing a song it's a reflection of my inner self as well as my social philosophy."

Being in a band is like being in any other relationship. You sometimes doubt the motivations or sincerity of the people you're involved with. You sometimes wonder what manner of substances and unfortunate string of events brought you together. Any doubts Tom might have had about the live wire with the cascading dreadlocks fronting his new band, evaporated when he got a chance to read over a book of Zack's lyrics that included what would become "Take the Power Back" and "Bullet in the Head." "The real clincher was when I looked through his book of poems and lyrics. It was like I'd found an ideological brother. And it wasn't just paragraphs about Mao and Paraguay," Tom said to *Rolling Stone*. "It was great poetry."

As Rage continued to gel, the question for the band became, What did they need to do to get to what rap stars insistently and vaguely refer to as "a whole other level"? The common route for bands in this instance is to scrape together a couple hundred dollars and go to a studio owned by "this guy they know" and record a scratchy three-song demo that people who have seen the band live can verify "kinda even sounds like them."

Having been burned by a major label with Lock-Up, Tim said Tom urged the band not to wait around for the big boys to come knocking, insisting that Rage record a demo on their own and let it sell itself by word of mouth. "Businessman Tom Morello, cracking the whip," Tim joked to *Rolling Stone*. "I remember going, 'Man, we can stop at eight songs. Eight will be fine.' He's like, 'No, we need more. We need twelve.' And that's what we did."

By assembling the record on their own, Rage gave their rapidly increasing fan base something to take home from shows and play for their friends. And they also gave themselves a leg up on the millions of bands that start up each year and go fishing around for record deals. "We wrote fifteen songs, and recorded twelve of them in what was supposed to be a sixteen-track studio, but three of the tracks didn't work," Tom recalled in *Jersey Rocks*. "We did it quick and rough, and sold about five thousand copies of it at our shows and through the underground. The version of 'Bullet In the Head' that's on the first album was taken from that demo—it was one of those magic takes that you just aren't going to be able to re-create."

As record labels began to take notice of what the fans who were buying Rage's underground tape already knew, a bidding war began for their services. The guys in the ponytails and cell phones were picking up on something that had been done before but never on a large-scale commercial level. Run-D.M.C. had collaborated with Aerosmith, and Ice-T put a scare into the establishment by daring to blend a fierce gangsta attitude with satanic heavy metal in his band Body Count, a fright much of the Midwest is still trying to get over. Chino Moreno, lead singer of the Deftones, put his finger on what was different with Rage and why they struck such a resonant chord with audiences, in an interview with *Spin* magazine. "I was inspired by the conviction behind the music and the sincerity behind the lyrics. It's not like they were the first band [to mix hard rock and rap], but they were the first to do it right."

The persistently backward thinking of Zack's hometown of Irvine, California, gave him plenty of fodder for lyrics. In an interview with *Spin*, Rob "Cubby" Hayworth, a veteran of Zack's two earlier bands, Hard Stance and Inside Out, talked about some of the racism Zack encountered in day-to-day life. "When Rage was first starting, he was going to junior college and still working forty hours a week doing, like, social work with kids. I remember we went into a store once to buy a desk or something, and they were looking at him real nervous. Then they're like, 'Oh, we don't make deliveries,' trying to make us leave. I saw the effect that stuff had on Zack, it had an effect on me, too."

With the emergence of so many bands that favor the hybrid of rap and metal that Rage helped popularize, it's almost difficult to recall a time when the two genres weren't intertwined in some way, but when Rage began,

industry sages discouraged them from melding the two together. "There was this one powerful manager we talked
to. He didn't want to manage the band, but he liked us
and he sat down and tried to give us some advice," Tom
recalled in the *L.A. Times.* "He spelled it out just like I
was a little kid or something. He said there's no future in
this 'rap thing—it's got no melody, no hooks.' He said we
put on an exciting show but there was no way we were
going to sell records or have a career."

Rage believed in themselves, but at the time, the nay-
saying manager was right in saying that what they were
trying to do was unprecedented. In an interview with *Vibe,*
Tom explained the obstacles Rage saw blocking their path
to success. "We're a multiethnic band and that was completely alienating to radio stations at the time. Even though
we were hip-hop, we were a real live band instead of in-
troducing a DJ and samples. And then there was the political element, so it was kind of like three strikes [against
us] with regards to a commercial connection."

In signing with a major label, Rage Against the Machine
had made a conscious decision to try and spread their message as far and as wide as the long marketing arm of Sony
Music could reach. After having trouble on Geffen while
in Lock-Up, Tom Morello needed to be assured of Rage's
complete creative control before agreeing to walk down
that path again. Being burned by a major label once was
plenty. "The reason it was a no-brainer for us to sign with

a major label was because we were able to get contractually guaranteed 100-percent creative control over every aspect of our career—period," Tom asserted to *CDNow*. "Once that was out of the way, then I had no argument with being on a major."

Getting good terms from a major label is about as easy and safe a proposition as sauntering through a minefield and coming through unscathed, but when Rage pushed their chairs back from the negotiating table and laid their pens down, they walked away knowing they'd signed a deal that would ensure they would record several albums on Sony or be handsomely compensated for any unreleased work. "We said the company had to not only guarantee that we would be able to make three albums, but if they reneged on the deal, there were specific amounts of money they would have to pay the band if they didn't make album two or three," Tom commented to the *L.A. Times*. "And it was substantial amounts—enough to make us feel their commitment was genuine."

In an interview with *Vox*, Zack said being exposed to other bands with strong political messages that had recorded for major labels made him realize the indie approach he'd taken with Inside Out wasn't the only way to fly. "My first band, Inside Out, was signed to a small indie label and we were very happy touring the West and East Coasts. At that point—I was nineteen, twenty—I began to be really influenced by Bob Marley and Public Enemy and the Clash. I saw them as being able to use music as a way of opening up the spectrum of ideas." Tom summed it up succinctly in an interview with the *Chicago Tribune*. "There is a conflict but how I look at it is, basically, while I eagerly await the day the United States government goes down in flames, I still use the U.S. postal system to write propagandistic letters to my politically minded friends around the country."

Nestled comfortably in the belly of the beast, Rage set to work on the process of rotting the machine from the inside out. Not content merely to release a fiery first album, Rage took their volatility to a higher level and went ahead and printed instructions for assembling a Molotov cocktail on T-shirts they sold on tour. In an interview with Australian magazine *The Age,* Tom talked about the consequences of and reasons for taking this explosive step. "The only real trouble we've had was in France. We had to get out of the country before the authorities confiscated all of our stuff—and probably us. They took it pretty seriously over there. Other than that I've been really surprised that nowhere else has there been that kind of reaction to it, because it's pretty explicit on how to make and detonate the Molotov cocktail. I think that kind of thing is important. If people are not checking the *Anarchist Cookbook* out of the library anymore, they can always look at the back of a Rage Against the Machine T-shirt the next time civil disorder breaks out in the neighborhood."

Rage opened for Public Enemy that year, a band whose collaboration with Anthrax had planted the seed for what

Rage and others would later nurture into one of the largest genres of music in the late 1990s and into the new millennium. Chuck D's first contact with Rage came in the form of a cassette tape. "My first impression of them came from a demo they sent to me. They sent a cassette tape with a match taped to the outside. I was like, 'Oh shit, what the fuck is this?' I didn't have any signing power or company to move them to at the time and then they wound up signing with Epic; they did the right thing obviously." Soon after Chuck D got his incendiary introduction to the band, they were opening for him and Public Enemy out on tour. Watching from the wings, Chuck D caught some of Rage's earliest shows and his recollections from that time could very easily be slid into reviews today. Honed over time, the potential Chuck D saw then has been realized over years of practice. "They opened for us in 1992; it's very ironic that I'm opening up for them on this Confrontation Camp tour and that Public Enemy opened up for them a couple times last year. I dig everything they've done. . . . To me they're the best because they're saying something and it actually makes a lot of sense. They rock hard and not too many people want to come on after them. What Tom does on guitar is revolutionary, it's in its own realm. You got Zack rapping his ass off and Tim and Brad stay in the pocket like some of that James Brown shit."

By the time Rage finished touring in support of their debut, they had done what every band dreams of doing and the fewest of the few succeed in doing. They had sold millions of copies of their first record, toured the world playing with some of their favorite bands, and achieved international critical acclaim. Heady stuff for anybody. Back in Los Angeles Zack found himself grappling with a problem not many of us have the luxury of struggling with. It boiled down to trying to balance his sudden fame with the feeling that he was still the same person. The same kid Beto had forced to fast and the same kid that had dreamed of a world bigger than the myopic confines of Irvine could provide. In an interview with *Vox*, Zack outlined the difficulty inherent in becoming a public figure. "Well, I try to keep myself grounded, I really do. I have a very difficult time with my position as a result of the band's popularity. I'm at constant war with it. A person who has that much attention placed on them is destined to come into conflict with themselves at some point and I try my best to alleviate it entirely, although I'm sure I've been affected by it in some way."

With no dreads springing from his head, Tim enjoys a slightly lower profile than Zack. In an interview with *Alternative Press* Tim said that, initially, not being an instantly recognizable celebrity due to his band status was disappointing, but over time he's come to be grateful for the ability to take his fame à la carte, with the bad parts kept to the side. "People rarely ever come up to me and say, 'Hey, man, are you in Rage Against the Machine?' That happens a couple times a year. I used to bum out on that because everyone wants to be famous, but now I feel so lucky. I just do my thing one minute, and then I'll fly off somewhere and play to like eighty thousand people. How can that be bad?"

Although Tim was not plagued with the price of fame, Rage's surge into prominence did cause him to take a closer look at his role in the band and to assess his comfort level with being part of band so readily associated with politics, sometimes even more than with music. Socially concerned in his own right, Tim was forced to adapt to the fact that being a member of Rage meant being part of an entity as well-known for their stance on the Leonard Peltier case as they are for their R-A-W-K. "It kind of sucks," Tim told *Raygun*. "Because somehow the music has almost taken a back seat to the politics of the band. Me, personally? I'm totally into issues, but at the same time, it's hard for me, because I started playing bass because I wanted to play music, not because I wanted to be a politician."

When it comes to the blend of politics and music, Tom adopts the philosophy that nothing happens in a vacuum, meaning simply that you can express just as much by what you don't say as what's actually vocalized. "I believe that culture and politics are inextricably linked and that there is no such thing as apolitical music. Like it or not. Artists don't necessarily realize that and some choose not to look at it that way. Some are naive," Tom told *Raygun*. "But escapist music is very political in upholding the status quo. That culture shapes the social landscape and makes certain things okay. You may not hate gay people, but if ten of your favorite rap artists are constantly singing homophobic songs, it contributes to an atmosphere in which it's okay to dislike gay people."

The political aspect of things was old hat for Tom and Zack, each having spent a considerable amount of time and energy in becoming politically educated and aware. For Brad, though, playing with them was like a crash course in sociology, taught exclusively in grimy band rooms, cramped backstage areas in small clubs, and later on planes and the tour bus. In an interview with the Australian publication *The Age*, Brad talked about what the early days of the band were like for him. "When I first joined the band, my eyes were opened to so many things, and my philosophies were right in line. If you want to break it down to the basic human emotions, it's all about taking the frustration and anger and injustices in the world and having a release from them."

Most bands release their debut albums quietly. There's a record-release party, with posters and free drinks, they play a set, people clap, the industry types tell them they're going to go all the way, the parents are proud, and then everyone goes home. The band goes out on tour; there's some nice articles written about them, some mean ones. They make some friends, they meet some groupies, and they come to terms with how much it sucks to drive through Kansas, and then it's all quiet on the western front until the next record comes out. Rage came onto the scene the way they do everything, loudly. If the blistering tracks on the disc weren't enough, the noise of rock-critics stumbling over themselves to herald the New Big Thing pushed them over the top. *Billboard*'s Timothy White led the charge, boldly proclaiming, "On the strength of the album, they must be viewed as one of the most original and virtuosic new rock bands in the nation. . . . Rage Against the Machine generates the most beautifully articulated torrent of hardcore bedlam that one could imagine. And the hopes invested in these humming murals of urban din are equally visionary."

Ice-T mixed metal and hip-hop early on with his rock band Body Count and in a collaboration with Slayer for the *Judgment Night* soundtrack. In his view the rap/metal hybrid that Rage helped popularize caught on largely because metal and rap were never far apart to begin with. "If you listen to Slayer, they're not singing, it's rap. They sing words really, really fast. And if you listen to a rapper, it's always 'Rock the mike, rock on, rock the house, rock that shit.' *Rock.* You don't 'R&B' shit, you *rock* shit. So rock is an energy level and an aggressive way of going about dealing with a topic. . . . Either you're doing pop or rock. With pop you're playing what people want to hear, you sing along with America, that's pop. When you say fuck something, it's rock. It started off with pianos back in the day, Little Richard, you know. So it's always been joined together."

Jim Kerr, alternative editor for the trade publication *Ra-*

dio & Records, said Rage began doing things right as far back as selecting their name. By picking such a moniker, Kerr said, Rage made a pact with their fans. "One thing to mention about the band," said Kerr. "It sounds so basic but right from the start they named themselves Rage Against the Machine. The name of the band is like a promise to fans. It's almost like they came out with a statement that, 'We are going to be a counterculture force. We are going to be the revolution.' If their music hadn't been politically edgy, if it wasn't clear that they were standing their own ground and being revolutionary, they wouldn't have been true to their own name."

Ice-T selected Rage as his opening act for one of their first tours in support of their self-titled debut. Rage had come recommended by his DJ. Ice-T checked out their live show and by the end of the gig he knew he had his opening act. "I was like, 'Lemme see 'em, what's up with them?' I saw motherfuckers jumping in the air. They had like four songs and 'Killing in the Name' was one of 'em. I heard that motherfucker yell out, 'Fuck you, I won't do what you tell me' and I was like 'Oh, I love 'em.' And we took them with us to New York and went a few places with 'em. Rage is a good band and I know they're sincere about what they're saying. The good thing about Zack and them is that they know about their hip-hop connections. They know Chuck [D]'s their biggest fan. They know they're a true hybrid of hip-hop and rock. It's not like a lie, it's not fake. It's real and it always has been. It's an incarnation of hip-hop, a good example of how it can happen. It's perfect."

During Rage's tours, Zack quickly learned to capitalize on the band's stage time and presence to further expound on the band's message, just as he used to with Inside Out. At a February 2, 1993, gig at the Melody in Stockholm, Sweden, Zack gave a monologue on the U.S. military presence in the Middle East before tearing into "Bullet in the Head." "For hundreds of years America has sent people into the fuckin' Middle East in the name of freedom, in the name of democracy, and have murdered innocent women and children to rape, conquer, and divest them of their resources. Today the situation still stands and people are still being murdered in the name of freedom. Wake up to your powers as an individual and speak out and act against fucking imperialistic actions like this."

Even after signing with Epic, Rage still sometimes felt twinges of doubt about going along with the promotion process involved in hyping a record in the 1990s. As MTV outgrew its status as a cable oddity and emerged as a major player on the music scene, landing a video on the channel became the difference between a band that sold a decent amount of records and a band that could cruise to rock-god status. For a lot of bands, getting a chance to make a video is one big hoot and holler and there can never be enough cars, girls, and spandex pants. For Rage, though, deciding to make the video for "Freedom" came about after a lot of head-scratching and conferring. Zack in particular had his doubts, having grown up a huge fan of the ultra-indie D.I.Y. band Minor Threat. Zack worried about the cred issue and that the great media machine would subsume and water down their defiant message and neuter their political force. In their interview CD, Zack explained he felt it best that the band grow at a gradual level and not allow their message to be subverted.

"At the point we got into whether or not to use videos as a way to disseminate information, at first I was very opposed to it. I think ultimately it was the right decision to make them. What would have happened if we'd sold six seven million copies of the record. Would actions of the band have been taken with the same emphasis? I don't think so. At times that's where me and Tom don't agree, we have a different approach to things."

Rage chose to work with Peter Christopherson, formerly of Throbbing Gristle and currently of Coil, who had previously done clips for Nine Inch Nails and Ministry. As usual, Rage made full use of the opportunity to draw attention to a cause, in this case splicing scenes from the 1992 documentary film *Incident at Oglala*, which dealt directly with the situation that led to Leonard Peltier's imprisonment, with live footage from their shows. Rage hoped the video would generate sufficient attention to Peltier's plight to convince President Clinton to pardon the Indian activist, a hope that had not come to fruition as of this writing. In an interview with MTV, Zack explained his personal attachment to Peltier's case. "I'm a Chicano and my history is rooted in the indigenous peoples of this continent. A lot of what's happened to Leonard and his people is reflective of my history. Leonard Peltier is a political prisoner but he's much more than that. He symbolizes the continuance of the U.S. genocidal policy that's been perpetuated against the native peoples of this country."

Given Zack's specific vision for the message the video would convey, Christopherson's challenge in creating the clip centered on how to communicate the gist of a complicated legal situation such as Peltier's to an audience made up of apathetic teenagers with miniscule attention spans. "Rage are one of those bands that have strong ideas of what the song is about. They're one of the few bands that manage to combine political statements with entertainment. The song was always about Leonard Peltier. What they wanted to do was try and tell that story as coherently as possible and bring his situation to a wider public. At the time, his case was coming up for appeal and they wanted to try and help. I spoke to Zack, he was generally the person I dealt with in the band. All four videos I made for the band, it was Zack's concept and I brought it into the visual realm. He gave me details and told me more about what happened because he'd been researching the truth behind the news story. We wanted to tell the story as simply as possible but in a way that would be powerful."

In what would become a trademark of the videos Christopherson would do for the band, the clip featured color and black-and-white footage of live performances, different-sized text, bits of *Incident at Oglala*, odd camera angles, all flashing by at a speed slightly faster than the mind's eye can comfortably digest. This high-octane approach was intentional, according to Christopherson. "The medium of a music video doesn't lend itself to telling a complicated legal case. The viewing public don't have a lengthy attention span. We wanted to keep people interested and excited in the process of what we were doing, and what they're trying to say will sink in as well. Having different textures and different looks and all kinds of graphic approaches is a way to keep people interested for a really long time, or five minutes, which is a long time for people lying on the couch drinking a beer or whatever."

Rage's determination to perform the video live with an actual audience, instead of lip-synching on a soundstage caused Christopherson to work in an unorthodox manner. "It was challenging in terms of editing," Christopherson told MTV. "But it's indicative of their dedication—it's more important for them that their audience can see that they're being genuine [than for the video to be perfectly synched]. In the end, it made the video stronger. What you see is the real thing."

While most bands use their first big tour as a chance to see just how ridiculous a backstage rider they can put together, or as an opportunity to meet the eager groupies that linger longingly at the foot of the stage, Rage had a different agenda. Recognizing the power personal contact has when trying to get across some of the complex political ideas Rage espouses, Zack made a habit of chatting to fans after the show and calmly explaining concepts he'd screamed from the stage only hours earlier. "We were in Detroit and Zack was holding a political discussion in the parking lot with fifteen kids," said Rage's A&R man Michael Goldstone in an interview with *Rolling Stone*. "And he was bummed out that the show was four thousand kids and he was only talking to fifteen. I said, 'Yeah, but those fifteen kids will tell fifteen other kids, and those will tell fifteen more kids.' "

Brad's practice of playing backwards at early shows nearly led to a disastrous onstage dustup. In a chat on Rage's official Web site, Tom talked about the gig gone wrong. "Years ago we were playing a show at the Hollywood Palladium and my guitar rig shorted out. I was left standing there with a dead guitar in my hands. This was during a phase of our career when Brad was playing with his drum set facing away from the audience. So I threw down my guitar and jumped up on the drum riser to help Brad finish the tumultuous end of 'Bullet in the Head' by whacking on a cymbal. When I jumped up on the riser, Brad wheeled around and thought that I was attacking him and tried to fight me in the middle of the song! I was shocked and declined to fight him, but by that time both the guitar player and the drummer had stopped playing and the song came to a horrible, pathetic whimpering conclusion as Zack and Tim turned in bewilderment and dismay to look at us squaring off while the crowd stood, mouths agape."

Other than this near-fisticuffs, Rage completed their first cycle in the music business successfully, having completed an album, endured an endless series of interviews, and toured the world without a hitch—but in the coming months it would only be the strength of that freshman year that would provide incentive to battle through an extended sophomore slump.

A good song should make you wanna tap your foot and get with your girl. A great song should destroy cops and set fire to the suburbs. I'm only interested in writing great songs.

—Tom Morello, *Alternative Press*

Touring completed, logic suggested it would be time to begin work on a second record, but this would not be as simple as it sounds. Sometime during the whirlwind of tours, benefits, and interviews the lines of communication needed to keep Rage moving in the same direction had gone down and no one had any real idea if they were ever going to come back up. The band had done a great job of establishing themselves on a global level but along the way, they had misplaced the electricity that had jolted them the first time they jammed. With the band at loggerheads, it looked to some, including some in the band, that they might be headed for Splitsville, U.S.A. Instead Rage went to Atlanta.

In an interview with *Rolling Stone* Tom explained why the band packed up and headed to the Southland. "There was no musical or personal communication going on. We were unable to agree on anything—to write music or

choose a T-shirt design. Our A&R guy, Michael Goldstone, said, 'Let's get rid of every distraction. You guys live
in a house down there. Either write a record or don't be a
band anymore.' It was, like [MTV's] *Real World* times ten."

Exactly what happened at Rage's aborted attempt at a
recording session in Atlanta will likely remain locked away
in the band members' mental archives but all involved admit those were some tense times. The band moved into a
house in Atlanta in the winter of 1994–95, thinking they
would live there while they recorded *Evil Empire*. The
sophomore slump is a well-documented phenomenon but
the difficulties went deeper than simply trying to record a
follow-up to a hugely successful debut. Rage's varied influences had served them well on their first album, as they
created an aggressive and fluid album that melded the genres of rap and rock, but in Atlanta tempers flared as ideas
of what the next record should sound like clashed. With
several years gone since they last wrote a record together,
Rage found themselves with differing visions for the second
record, and enough in-fighting to make the label and each
other wonder if it would ever get made.

"I was certainly strained by the personal tension. . . .
Number one, I was really trying to insure that we weren't
writing another Sabbath-meets-rap record," Zack told the
Alternative Press. "That was really fucking important to me.
Number two was this: We were too busy with what we were
doing to address the problems that we had with each other.

It was three years of touring and never speaking about any real personal concerns."

Brad's memories of the time in Atlanta have nothing to do with music and everything to do with the personal difficulties the band battled through. He offered his version of that tumultuous time in *Modern Drummer*. "We wrote twenty songs in Atlanta and I can't even remember them. I remember letting off fireworks in the neighborhood and pushing the refrigerator out on the front lawn — stuff that had nothing to do with music. It was a time for getting personal stuff out."

As with many bands, the partial root of the dispute within Rage was about ego. Whose vision for the band is the right one? Who is doing most of the work? Who is getting the credit? Citing internal differences acknowledges the tensions present, but doesn't say where they are coming from. Almost to a man, Rage kept mum on the specifics of their winter of discontent but Zack did admit in an interview with *Kerrang!* that part of his frustration stemmed from the fact that he felt he wasn't getting his due from his bandmates. "I didn't feel my contribution was recognized among the four of us. At that point I had written and arranged half of Rage's music, yet still felt as a songwriter I wanted props of recognition from the others. It's not about self-aggrandizement or money. I just wanted recognition."

Tempers flared to the point that members privately wondered if Rage could ever patch up their differences and record. In an interview with *Musician*, Brad said there was a time he thought a breakup was more likely than not. "I thought it might happen. But there was always a voice in my head asking why. There was such animosity that breaking up felt like the easy way out. It'll always be day to day. I hope we can stay together because we haven't reached our potential yet."

Accounts on how long Rage stayed in Atlanta vary from four weeks to five months, but everyone agrees it was the lowlight of Rage's career. While the band squabbled, Goldstone squirmed. The genesis of the first record came together before Rage had a record deal and the second looked to come out around the time My Bloody Valentine's follow-up to *Loveless* hits stores. Goldstone knew Rage clicked when they were on, but he couldn't find a way to flick the switch. What once had looked to be a dominating force in the world of rock for years to come, seemed to be imploding before the band could fully realize their abilities. One record and out. Goldstone recalled his dilemma in *Rolling Stone*. "My frustration was, 'How can I be involved with a band this great and not figure out a way to get them to make records?' The differences made it difficult to move the process along but it was the conflict that made the band so great."

In the end, the time spent in Atlanta proved valuable only insofar as it highlighted the fact that Rage is a band made up of four individuals with different visions and hopes for the band, and any successful collaboration is the result of communication and compromise. "I wish I could say there were a lot of positive things that came out of it, but there weren't," Zack told *Spin*. "Look, I don't particularly care for [Black] Sabbath, and Tom doesn't particularly care for a lot of the hip-hop riffs that I come up with. But the two, when fused together, make something unique."

The breakup that seemed to be lurking around every corner of the Atlanta house never actually surfaced but when Rage left the state of Georgia, they left with a bitter taste in their mouths and came back to California no closer to completing a new record than when they had left.

If things weren't tumultuous enough, it was during this period that Rage fired manager Warren Entner, who declined comment on his relationship with the band. With no contact from him for a whole year before the issues in Atlanta, the dealbreaker was when Rage learned that management had neglected to answer their fan mail. Rage swiftly dispatched Entner and mailed fans on their mailing list their cover of N.W.A's "Fuck Tha Police" as a means of appeasement. In an interview with *Musician* magazine, Tom explained the decision to dismiss Entner. "We figured that since he obviously wasn't interested in us, we'd just part ways. He'd been an absent manager, not a malicious manager. Then after doing nothing for us, he wanted a million dollars to be let out of his contract."

Once the drama had played itself out, the band found themselves at Cole Rehearsal Studios in Hollywood, working with producer Brendan O'Brien, who they had met when he did some remixes of singles from the first album. Paired with O'Brien they began recording the songs that would become the supple fruit of some bitter infighting. Rather than rent out a state-of-the-art studio, Rage opted to adapt their rehearsal space to meet their needs, jury-rigging the room to get it up to snuff. "Why spend two thousand dollars a day in some fancy recording studio trying to re-create the great vibe that we have right here? . . ." Tom pointed out to MTV. "So we literally knocked a hole in the wall, rented the room across the hall and ran the wires over the hallway." Zack chimed in, "We weren't going to go in and play in a studio that had no environment whatsoever. You get in some of those places and it's like you're walking into a dentist's office. I've had my teeth cleaned, thanks a lot, I don't want to do that."

With the studio rigged per their specifications it was time to do what they'd failed to do in Atlanta: Write songs. For some bands the songwriting process is pretty simple. The star of the show tells everyone else what to play and they learn how to play it. Rage takes a more democratic approach, with everyone offering input and writing their own parts. In an interview with *Launch*, Tim described the process. "We write the music before. We're riff-rock without question. We get together, come up with riffs, hook them with other riffs we've done, and then arrange the songs. We'll hear the vocals most times, and the chorus, and then we give the songs to Zack to be able to spend time to write the words."

Lyrically, the new songs reflected what was going on in the world at the time. As Zack examined the motivations of the U.S. government for declaring war on Iraq and the reactions of certain members of the talk-show media, a kernel of indignation began to form. Realizing that some of the same people involved in Watergate and the Iran-Contra affair were hosting talk shows gave Zack ample ammunition. "When I wrote 'Vietnow' I had been driving around L.A. listening to AM radio, to these Nazis' right-wing, twenty-four-hour war against poor people," Zack told Chuck D in *Rip* magazine. "I'm sitting there tripping. I mean, these motherfuckers are war criminals! G. Gordon Liddy . . . motherfucking Oliver North was in Nicaragua killing people. Now he's a war hero and on the radio, and come election time he's having a major impact for a swing to the right."

Zack's pointed raps, Brad and Tim's rhythm in lockstep, and Tom's tweaking his guitar all emerged as staples of the Rage sound with *Evil Empire*. Tom takes a scientific approach to dredging up the squawks, squeals, and shrieks he conjures out of his guitar. Just as a chemist collects data during an experiment, Tom plays mad professor and keeps a chart of unusual sounds he discovers as he plays guitar and takes notes that remind him how he made them.

"Most of what's on the Noise Chart comes from accidents during soundcheck or the live set," Tom told *Guitar World* in his 1997 Guitarist of the Year interview. "Like I'd forget to turn the delay knobs back from where they are for 'Vietnow,' and—uh-oh—I'm in the middle of 'Bullet in the Head' and the knobs should be different, but let's go for it. It's those little bends in the road where you discover new sounds."

Completing *Evil Empire* was like arriving at a hard-fought and uneasy truce. Rage's debut had featured a new act surely stepping into the spotlight; *Evil Empire* showcased a band just past a fork in the crossroads, still not quite certain they went in the right direction. In talking about the record with *Kerrang!*, Tom takes a diplomatic tone, suggesting that *Evil Empire* was okay with everyone but not adored by anyone. "*Evil Empire* was a different album from *Rage Against the Machine*. The songs on the original record were written in about the first month we met each other, and there was a spontaneity to them. *Evil Empire* was a record where we found a course between our very different musical tastes to make a record that was compelling both musically and lyrically and a record that we could all be proud of, and finding that course took some time." All of which makes recording an album sound about as pleasant and fun as open-heart surgery.

Rage had made a bold statement with their first album cover by using, front and center, the infamous picture of a monk setting himself ablaze in protest over the occupation of South Vietnam. The self-immolating monk clearly served as a metaphor for what Rage were doing, igniting themselves in the hopes of igniting others. For their second album they opted for a less fiery approach, selecting a drawing of a smirking white kid wearing an *Evil Empire* jersey. The name *Evil Empire* had been inspired by a speech given by Ronald Reagan during the closing days of the Cold War, where he condemned the Soviet Union with the moniker. Zack explained the symbolism behind the second cover in an interview with *Rip* magazine. "When you consider the atrocities we've committed in the late twentieth century you know that you can easily flip that on its head and apply it directly to the United States, so that's where we got the title. Imagewise, we got this Eagle Scout–looking white kid who's smiling 'cause he's in control, but if you look real closely you'll see there's fear in his eyes as well. He's realized that all this shit he perpetuated on people is coming back."

As much as seeing the band nearly unravel in Atlanta had rattled Rage, the time spent in the doldrums was far outweighed by the thrill of playing live, or the occasional boost of encouragement from an unlikely source. On a European tour with Neil Young, the legendary singer-songwriter took a moment to praise Rage, offering unsolicited props that Brad told *Modern Drummer* helped remind everyone that they were on the right track.

"We'd been having a few rough days in the band, and Neil came in the dressing room and said what a great band he thought we were. I never thought he would really like what we do, but he was totally into us. He thought our chemistry was really great. Neil Young doesn't need to kiss anyone's ass. He must mean it. So that's nice to here when you're going through rough personal times. It helped."

Despite all the infighting and the fear of breaking apart, *Evil Empire* became a success both critically and commercially. The record went multiplatinum in less than a year and "Bulls on Parade," "Tire Me," and "People of the Sun" each were nominated for a Grammy, with "Tire Me" ultimately winning Rage one of those little gold record-players in the Best Metal Performance category. It nearly tore the band apart, but when all was said and done, *Evil Empire* proved to be a successful second record and the understandings achieved during its recording laid a foundation that made the idea of a third record and beyond a viable one.

When it came time to shoot videos for the album, Rage once again turned to director Peter Christopherson. Building on the rapid-fire media-blitz technique he had orchestrated with their "Freedom" video, Christopherson used similar methods in treatments for "Bulls on Parade" and "People of the Sun." Christopherson explained the concepts behind the two clips.

"For 'Bulls on Parade' the whole band wanted to make a piece of footage reminiscent of political footage from different times. They deliberately wanted to use different eras of style of political messages. They purposely wanted the kids shown in the video to be of different races, creeds, and colors. And the scene when they get to the top of the hill and they're pulling up the American-flag picture looks very much like the photo of the soldiers at Iwo Jima. At the same time there's a very strong anti-authoritarian message. The words speak for themselves and Rage wanted the video to reflect that. 'People of the Sun' was more specifically about the situation in Chiapas. We wanted to have information but we didn't want to bury people in a bunch of facts. All the information comes in the form of blipverts, pages of information that flick through really quickly. We wanted to have a caption at the front of the video saying, 'Start your VCR now,' so people could record it and then watch it at a slower speed to get all the messages. It's a bit like a trick street musicians do where they flick through the pack of cards and they have you pick one at random. One card's rigged to be held a frame longer. It's the same with the information in the video, some of the bits are held for a frame and a half longer than the rest, so you can get a sense of what these things are about and hopefully some people investigate on their own."

Christopherson said his extensive work with Rage was satisfying artistically because it allowed him to expand the idea of what videos are for and can be. "You have to understand that very few videos have an agenda and very few videos have an idea other than to show the artist in a cool and original light. It's a shame because to make five minutes of film for a video is the same as making five minutes of a film for a movie, or for a broadcast. They all perform the same job. Videos now days tend to abandon efforts to do anything except be cool. When I have the opportunity to work on a video that has a political idea behind it and that says things over and above just 'We're a cool band,' I have to decide what's important in the idea and try to find the best way to put it across and the most succinct."

When you take an extreme stance of any kind, there's bound to be a backlash. When the stance involves politics the stakes are raised even higher. The greatest freedom fighters of the twentieth century, people like Gandhi and Dr. Martin Luther King Jr., were gunned down in their prime, due largely to their strident and unpopular political views. Now, we do have to tone it down a bit because Rage is still a just rock band and aren't leading millions of Indians on freedom marches or spending nights in Alabama jails, but their far left–leaning position has attracted a great deal of attention from law enforcement, sometimes even for acts as simple as announcing a tour. Take for instance when Rage teamed up with the Wu-Tang Clan. The tour began innocuously enough but the wheels fell off almost before they got rolling.

"The Wu-Tang tour was dramatic to say the least. The combination of our politics and a rap group terrified the authorities," Tom told *Kerrang!* "We managed to intercept a memorandum meant for a local sheriff's department in Colorado and it talked about anti-police sentiments and the blackness of Wu-Tang. They then tried to file injunctions, but none of them were successful thanks to the First Amendment."

Going into the tour, Rage was excited at the prospect of touring with the Wu-Tang. Among the most innovative hip-hop outfits around, Wu-Tang Clan floored hip-hop heads with their debut record, *36 Chambers*, an album that helped redefine the medium. Then, in a brilliant marketing scheme, the various members released solo albums on a wide range of labels, meaning that any given time some record label was promoting some Wu-Tang–related album. In describing what he liked about Wu-Tang in an interview with the *Chicago Tribune*, Tom touched on many points that could easily apply to Rage as well. "If a group is going to save hip-hop, it's going to be the Wu-Tang Clan. They've stripped the form of the R&B-drenched, radio-pandering artifice and enjoyed enormous commercial success without aesthetic compromise." In many ways it should have been the ideal tour for Rage. The Lollapalooza crowd had caught on a few years back and there was no denying the metallic clout and fist-pumping fury of "Killing in the Name," but the hip-hop aspect of the band hadn't been fully recognized to that point. Playing to a mixture of their own fans and die-hard Wu-Tang devotees each night should have given Rage the perfect opportunity to highlight another aspect of their sound.

Although artistically the two bands were on the same path, their politics didn't align as smoothly, a fact that gave Rage some misgivings but ultimately Tom told *Rolling Stone* that Wu-Tang's repeated use of the word "bitch" among others wasn't going to be a dealbreaker. "We don't have an ideological litmus test you have to pass to share a stage with Rage. There are few groups filled with saints. Wu-Tang makes a lot of great music, but the misogynous content is something we're not into at all. It ruffles the Alan Alda side of my personality, but I'm not going to call off the tour."

In an eerie prognostication of what was to come, Zack actually forecasted the difficulties Rage would have, in an interview with *Rolling Stone* prior to the start of the tour. Describing why Rage and Wu-Tang would click, Zack predicted the trouble they would have later in the junket. "We're not going to play to the [mainstream]; we're going to hijack it. The tour is going to incorporate everything which the rich, wealthy classes in America fear and despise. Each of the twenty thousand people in the audience will be reminded of their independent political power. . . . America is filled with sections of racist conservatism, and they're misled in thinking that us or Wu-Tang are a threat to their communities. I expect we will run into problems somewhere in the country. Honestly, part of me hopes we do."

Beyond the meddling of law enforcement officials, additional tour snags were caused by the absence of Wu-Tang members at certain shows, a rumored assault backstage at the World Music Theater in the Tinley Park neighborhood of Chicago, and ended with the Wu-Tang Clan dropping off the bill midway through the arena-sized tour. The alleged assault led to a lawsuit but Tom said the Wu-Tang component of the tour had been a sinking ship well before the lawyers got involved. In an interview with *Addicted to Noise*, Tom said other factors led to Wu-Tang leaving the tour early. "Well, I was at Tinley Park and, I don't know, I didn't see anything going on. The dressing rooms are kind of in different corners. I have no idea. I think that it's pretty clear that whatever may have happened at Tinley Park had nothing to do with them dropping off the tour. I think it was that they had internal differences that they had to sort out and they couldn't do it on tour."

Losing Wu-Tang to that catchall cop-out for bands — "internal differences" — was disappointing, but with the distinct memory of Rage's time in Atlanta still fresh, Brad found a silver lining amid all the drama. "It was good for us," said Brad in an interview with *Alternative Press*. "It was so great having a band like that on tour with us because it kinda took the pressure off of us for a minute. It was like all of a sudden we could look at their bullshit and not our own."

Even after the Wu-Tang Clan dropped off, Rage had difficulties with law enforcement professionals. Prior to

Rage's arrival in George, Washington, for a show at the Columbia Gorge amphitheater, the local sheriff sought to block the performance, claiming that he'd heard from sheriffs in other towns that Rage were likely to incite the crowd to violence. Sheriff William Wiester filed a motion with Grant County Superior Court Judge Ken Jorgensen that termed the band "violent and anti–law enforcement," as well as "militant, radical and anti-establishment." The motion failed and the concert was allowed to proceed as scheduled with openers Atari Teenage Riot and the newly added Roots onboard. In an effort to diffuse things some, Tom called the local radio station ahead of time, urging fans to keep cool heads. Once there, Zack took over, offering his opinion on the whole snafu from onstage. "He has the nerve to call us violent when last year there were eighty thousand cases of police brutality filed against departments all over the country. This sheriff pig is poppin' off, poppin' off about how we're violent. Well, shit, he belongs to the most violent gang in U.S. history."

Pushing the envelope means controversy comes calling at all times and places, even in the generally innocuous forum of television appearances. Whoever scheduled Rage Against the Machine and Republican presidential candidate Steve Forbes on *Saturday Night Live* on the same night, April 13, 1996, either had a much better sense of humor than the skit writers or a secret love of the kind of chaos that causes TV disasters. Pairing the Marxist rock band with the conservative billionaire looked bad on paper and was worse in practice. Over the years *SNL* has built up a reputation for unflinching cutting-edge humor, and served as a springboard onto the national scene for comedians such as John Belushi and Eddie Murphy. In the early and mid-1990s the show's slump was a thing of national record. The jokes lagged, the laughs died, and people stopped watching. Still, playing on *Saturday Night Live* continued to carry some cachet for bands. In its heyday, performers like Elvis Costello used galvanizing performances on the show as a springboard to greater notoriety and acclaim.

Eager to capitalize on the national forum, producer and band pal Brendan O'Brien crept onstage a mere twenty seconds before Rage were set to go live and duct taped a pair of upside-down American flags over the band's equipment. Tom explained the symbolism of the flags in an interview with Rock Out Against Censorship. "The inverted flags represented our contention that American democracy is inverted when what passes for democracy is an electoral choice between two representatives of the privileged class. America's expression is inverted when you're free to say anything you want to say until it upsets a corporate sponsor. Finally this was our way of expressing our opinion of the show's host, Steve Forbes."

A *Saturday Night Live* staffer ripped the flags down just as the ultraconservative Forbes introduced the slightly left-leaning Rage to the American public, as the band tore into

"Bulls on Parade." When a shredded Old Glory was found in Forbes's dressing room, *SNL* pulled the plug on a planned second song by the band, fearing further subversive activity. In retrospect, their fears were well founded, as Tom recalled in *Alternative Press*. "I was talking to Zack about Plan B before we played. I suggested that he mention somewhere during the song that General Electric, who owns NBC, made weapons that committed war crimes in the Gulf. . . . If they only had a clue about some of the things we were thinking of doing, they probably would have thanked us for only turning flags upside down."

As Brad recalled in *Modern Drummer*, Rage was enraged at first, but after a while came to the conclusion that their high-profile ejection from the show may actually have served to highlight their cause better than the upside-down flags would have done. "We were like, 'This sucks.' We went back to the dressing room to figure out what to play for the second song. As we were deciding what to do, one of the big guys from the show came down and asked us to leave the building. We told him to shove it, and then we left. They said they didn't want us dressing up their set. But what if those flags had been painted on our equipment? In retrospect it got more publicity by them doing that than if we had just done our thing."

Getting kicked off the show was only part of the picture. Angered that the band had been asked to censor certain lyrics out of deference to Forbes and his family, Tom cried corporate conspiracy in a press release issued by Rock Out

Against Censorship that addressed their aborted appearance. "*SNL* censored Rage, period. They could not have sucked up to the billionaire more. The thing that's ironic is *SNL* is supposedly this cutting-edge show, but they proved they're bootlickers to their corporate masters when it comes down to it. They're cowards. It should come to no surprise that GE, which owns NBC, would find 'Bullet' particularly offensive. GE is a major manufacturer of U.S. planes used to commit war crimes in the Gulf War, and bombs from those jets destroyed hydroelectric dams which killed thousands of civilians in Iraq."

Although members of the cast apologized to the band after the show, Brad told *Spin* getting booted early added insult to injury because the show itself wasn't up to snuff. "It would have been another thing if that show had been really funny. But I could eat a bowl of alphabet soup with orange juice and shit out better skits than I saw that night."

Rage landed a slot on the main stage of Lollapalooza '93. The previous year they'd played a two-day slot on the second stage, at Irvine Meadows, in southern California, in what was more or less a hometown show. It was a reunion of sorts for Tom, as Libertyville's Adam Jones of Tool and Maureen Herman of Babes in Toyland were on board with their bands, as well as Dinosaur Jr., Fishbone, Arrested Development, Alice in Chains, and Primus.

Still a relatively new phenomenon at that time, Lollapalooza was a celebration of all things alternative, with booths that featured everything from political pamphlets to piercings. Kids ate vegetarian food, got tattoos, and signed petitions circulated by people bent on saving the world. In keeping with the college-freshman optimism and "We're gonna make a difference" attitude, at a show in Philadelphia Rage made the clothing-optional statement of stepping out onstage naked except for a strip of black tape over their mouths.

"We stood on the stage for about fourteen minutes, naked, just letting the guitar and bass feed back, with the letters PMRC written in big, black letters, one on each band member's chest, with black electrical tape over our mouths. . . ." Tom recounted to *Spin*. "People at the show were wildly enthusiastic for the first five minutes, then they realized it wasn't going to be a feel-good protest, then the second five minutes, they were silent, waiting for the rock to begin, then the last five minutes they were actively hostile, very uncomfortable, and upset."

Championed by none other than Tipper Gore, wife of then U.S. senator Al Gore, the Parents' Music Resource Center applied pressure on the major record labels in the mid-1980s to put warning labels on albums that contained what was deemed foul language or vulgar content. Opposition to their efforts was fierce, to the point that Frank Zappa testified against their proposed legislation in the Senate, and there was a general fear in the industry that a cause like this could snowball. In an interview with *Option* magazine, Zappa explained how a PMRC-backed bill in the Maryland state senate could have easily meant jail time for simply wearing a T-shirt. "To give an example of how ridiculous this bill was, under this bill you were not allowed to advertise pornography. So let's say that somebody decided that a Mötley Crüe album was obscene. If you were wearing a T-shirt that says Mötley Crüe on it you would be advertising pornography. You could be fined $1,000 and/or go to jail for a year."

Rage's silent, pantsless protest directed a great deal of attention to the anti-censorship cause as well as the naked guys onstage, but guitarist Mike Muir of Suicidal Tendencies, who had toured with Rage early on, cast doubts on the band's motivations. "There's a fine line between making a political statement and trying to add to your financial statement," Muir retorted in *Spin*. "Why is it [that reports of the Philly PMRC incident were] in every paper in the industry? 'Because we sent a press release out.' And who the fuck fucked with you? Oh, the PMRC? They don't even fuckin' exist in the real world anymore."

Brad admitted to *Rolling Stone* that the band had an ulterior motive, but asserted it was not related to finances or public relations. The drummer said that with Zack's voice gone, Rage decided to capitalize on the chance to address the anti-censorship cause, the very thing that allows them to voice their strident political views publicly.

"It was either that or do a half-ass show. We were in Philadelphia—the birthplace of American independence—and thought, 'We need to take advantage of this.' 'Is everybody cool with being naked?' 'Yeah, yeah, yeah.' After about ten minutes people realized all they were going to hear was feedback. I got hit with a lighter, some other shit people were throwing. I remember my hand sliding from my waist down to my private parts, going, 'Please don't hit there.' "

Tim told *Musician* magazine that while onstage in Philadelphia he worried he wasn't being properly represented under the circumstances. It wasn't so much that justice was getting short shrift, but that accounts of the day might not give him proper credit in a more basic way. "Want me to be perfectly frank with you? The size of my penis—that's what was going through my mind in Philadelphia. It looked like I'd just stepped out of the ocean. I swear to God, it's bigger than that. So I was thinking, 'I wish I'd worn boxer shorts before instead of briefs, because briefs kinda like constrict me. I took them off and it was this . . . half-roll of nickels."

While well-aware of the higher purpose Rage's nakedness was serving, Brad told *Modern Drummer* that he, too, had some more fundamental concerns that had nothing to do with the triumph of making a blunt anti-censorship statement. "I was thinking about how the wind felt underneath my scrotum, what the people in the front were thinking, and all the cameras flashing and what they were going to be thinking as they developed their film. Actually, doing that was no big deal. It didn't freak me out. That's how we all came into the world. It's a liberating thing."

At the New Orleans stop of the Lollapalooza tour, Tim and Brad got a free ride downtown from the New Orleans police after Tim attempted to prevent the cops from giving a homeless black man the shakedown. He was arrested on what he claimed to be an unfounded charge of public intoxication. At the next day's show, Tom's mom exacted a measure of revenge, leading the throng in a throaty cheer of "Fuck the New Orleans police." In retrospect, Tim told *Spin*, the lessons learned were limited. "The only thing the experience did for me is make me realize I seriously cannot stand police at all. I'm going to vocalize to any cop I ever see that I hate him and wish he was dead, based solely on the fact that he's a cop. I promise you that one day, maybe it'll be ten years from now, I'll go, 'I'm even with police.' I'll go, 'I can't tell you what I did, but I can tell you that I'm even.' "

Brad's memories of Lollapalooza are bittersweet at best. A series of personal traumas weighed heavily on him at a time that should have been a great one for him and the band. In an interview with *Spin*, Brad talked about the devastating series of events that had led up to the Lollapalooza tour. "Lollapalooza was a little strange, because three days before the tour my dad was killed, halfway through the tour a friend committed suicide, and [band friend] Brett Kantor was murdered."

Although the Lollapalooza tour was marred by arrests and deaths, the publicity generated by the naked show in Philadelphia catapulted Rage into the national spotlight and made the band a household name for the first time.

We see our music as part of a cultural battlefield. We want to cut through the bullshit the system slams down young people's throats. We are trying to present an alternative view of the world. Rage Against the Machine want to build a bridge between the music and the movement.
—Tom Morello, *Socialist Worker*

The biggest divide between Rage Against the Machine and bands that think being political means wearing a Rock the Vote button in concert is concrete action: Putting your money where your mouth is. Putting up or shutting up. Shitting or getting off the pot. (Fill in your favorite cliché here.) Even before Rage collected its first platinum record, the band was working with the Anti-Nazi League in Europe to coordinate a benefit concert. Concerned that the political climate in England was taking a stormy right turn for the worse, Rage followed in the footsteps of the Clash and organized benefits to try and stem the rising tide of indifference. Joined by Senser, Headswim, Green Apple Quickstep, and Lush, Rage played the Brixton Academy in September of 1993 and succeeded in raising money for the Anti-Nazi League and publicizing an anti-Nazi march set for the sixteenth of that month.

"The National Front of England had just elected its first member to Parliament, and we found a great deal of apathy there, as opposed to fifteen years ago when the Clash was out there supporting the miners' strike," Tom informed *Alternative Press*. "We did a couple of shows that culminated in street action where the kids in Brixton were demonstrating to the Nazis that their fear tactics wouldn't work. We played a small part in that."

A little over a year later, with a pair of headlining slots for Rock for Choice already completed, Rage played Latinpalooza — a benefit for the Leonard Peltier Defense Fund, Para Los Niños, and United Farm Workers. Joining them on the bill were Cypress Hill, Little Joe y la Familia, Lighter Shade of Brown, Fobia, and Thee Midnighters. Little Joe of the Grammy-winning Little Joe y la Familia, grew up as a migrant farm worker in Temple, Texas, and, having played numerous benefits for the United Farm Workers over the years, took the cause to heart. "I picked cotton through my seventeenth birthday and started playing music when I was fifteen. I know exactly what it feels like, the low wages, the hard work, and the discrimination you have to go through. People don't realize that the food we eat is really harvested and planted by people that work under such terrible conditions." Little Joe praised Rage for their involvement, adding that for a band with their high profile, the stakes are raised. "To lend a helping hand and to be willing to do that without fear they'll lose their status or fame — they should be commended. I commend any artist that's willing to do that. Thank heaven for bands that are willing to do that. It's very much like Willie Nelson [with Farm Aid]."

The cause hit home for Zack as well. While he personally had never worked in the fields as a migrant worker, his grandfather had, and his father Beto once made murals for the United Farm Workers. In an interview with the Spanish-language magazine *Frontera*, Zack talked about the impact his grandfather's experience had on him. "My Sinaloan grandfather was a revolutionary fighter who fought in the Mexican Revolution. My grandfather went to the United States as an economic migrant. He was an agricultural laborer in Silicon Valley, California. His working days lasted from fifteen to sixteen hours daily, sweating and subjected to poverty. . . . I see his experience reflected in the testimonies of the Zapatistas, the indigenous peasant rebels who struggle every day to make a living."

Beyond high-profile benefits and addressing audiences on specific issues, Rage consistently offers materials to fans that will help them educate themselves about current affairs and issues of interest. In the liner notes for both *Evil Empire* and *The Battle of Los Angeles*, Rage included addresses and Web sites for organizations such as the Anti-Nazi League and the legal defense committees for Leonard Peltier and Mumia Abu-Jamal. On their official Web site, (www.ratm.com) Rage take it a step further and offer the same addresses and Web sites, as well as a reading list that

includes the political writings of authors such as Noam
Chomsky and Karl Marx, and thought-provoking fiction
by writers such as James Joyce and John Steinbeck. In an
interview with MTV, Zack said the reading list was designed for people who grew up in the same way he did,
angry but uncertain which way to turn. "I certainly didn't
find any of those books at my University High School library. Many of those books may give people new insight
into some of the fear and pain they might be experiencing
as a result of some of the very ugly policies that the government is imposing upon us right now. Putting them
back in touch . . . with realizing that their direct partici-
pation in events right now can affect history." In addition,
the Freedom Fighter of the Month section of the Rage
Web site highlights a different young activist each month,
singling them out in their community and acknowledging
the work that they do. Ironically, not all of those so hon-
ored have been pleased to be picked. In an interview with
Spin magazine, Alex Zwerdling of Middlebury College in
Vermont, spoke of his mixed feelings about being picked
as Freedom Fighter of the Month in November of 1999
for his work with United Students Against Sweatshops. "I
was a little embarrassed, to be honest. And at the risk of
pissing off the band, there was the issue of them being anti-
corporation and anti–whatever else, but they're on Sony, a
massive multinational corporation. I did get some shit from
activist friends on campus. And maybe [Rage] aren't as
pure as they'd like to be, or as they'd like to look, but

they're trying to give us a voice, and we're trying to give workers a voice. Now they seem to be bringing the message in a more informed way."

Not everyone sees Rage's efforts through the dubious eyes of the idealistic young Mr. Zwerdling. Among the less cynical listeners out there is guitarist Wayne Kramer, formerly of the MC5, who told the *Chicago Tribune* that he sees Rage and their vigilant pursuit of justice for the overlooked and underprivileged as part of a long line of activism in America that goes back hundreds of years. "The stuff that Rage Against the Machine is talking about is essentially what the MC5 were talking about, that all liberals and revolutionaries have talked about in this country going back to Thomas Paine. And it's not glamorous or sexy or exciting. We're talking about justice, education, health care, and jobs—the fundamental building-blocks of civilization."

What makes what Rage tries to do unique is the time frame they're working in. British folk singer Billy Bragg, who has made two records with Wilco using the lyrics of noted singer-songwriter Woody Guthrie, said the older generation of songwriters had an easier time reaching people. "In defense of Rage, both me and Woody grew up in a society of politics where the two sides were opposed to one another. Right versus left, so it was a bit easier. In some ways Rage is trying to make political music in a vacuum. The fact that they're trying to do it deserves a lot of credit."

One of the higher-profile causes championed by Rage is that of Leonard Peltier, an American Indian activist convicted of murdering two FBI agents. By aligning themselves with Peltier's cause, Rage joined a list of backers that includes the Dalai Lama, Archbishop Desmond Tutu, the Reverend Jesse Jackson, Robert Redford, Amnesty International, European Parliament, Italian Parliament, Belgian Parliament, and the National Congress of American Indians. Despite the international coalition of support, Peltier remains jailed on charges of murder stemming from a shoot-out on June 26, 1975, that left two FBI agents and one Native American dead. Peltier fled to Canada to avoid prosecution but was ultimately extradited back to the States to stand trial. Initially four men were charged with the murders, but charges against the others were dismissed and Leonard alone was convicted of first-degree murder and sentenced to two consecutive life terms. The International Office for the Defense of Leonard Peltier claims the evidence that got Leonard Peltier convicted was spotty and circumstantial at best, and at one point during the appeals process the Eighth Circuit Court of Appeals termed the FBI's investigation as "a clear abuse of the investigative process," and yet ruled against giving Leonard a new trial.

Wanting to assist with the expensive legal process involved in appealing Peltier's case and bringing attention to his cause, Rage worked to organize a benefit concert, For the Freedom of Leonard Peltier, at California State University of Dominguez Hills, putting together a bill that included the Beastie Boys, Cypress Hill, the classic L.A. punk band X, Mother Tongue, and the Stanford Prison Experiment. The $75,235.91 raised by the benefit went to the Leonard Peltier Defense Fund, which helps to pay Peltier's substantial legal fees.

Bassist John Doe of X talked about the show. "I think we got involved because Rage are X fans. We also played a Rock for Choice benefit with Rage. They asked us to play. My recollections are everything going to shit when the Beasties played. They went off and people went nuts. I felt sorry for Cypress Hill, that they had to play next. I remember sitting by the soundboard while Rage was going on and the entire floor of that stadium was like it was boiling, with people as the boiling water."

Doe added that Rage's kind of activism requires diligence both as an artist and as a crusader; as an artist, to remain innovative; and as an activist, to take each step you say you're going to. "If you don't try to let people see the other side of what the media tells you, you're missing out on a huge part of being an artist. It has to be done in way that's not just preaching. I think Rage walks a fine line — they're a little preachy but they've got the music to balance it out. You can teach people by example. If that example is being socially aware and politically aware and responsible, then your audience is going to mimic that and accept it as something they could do and should do. But if you're going to talk the talk, you gotta walk the walk. You've got to contribute your own money and own time and effort to

those causes. I think that's what advantage is in the func-
tion of music with politics. It seduces people into activism.
If you hear a song that's kinda preachy, you don't care if
it fucking rocks; it's like giving kids a little sugar with medicine."

The "preachy" charge gets leveled at Rage a lot and it's
true that freedom movements and execution stays aren't
what keeps the kids in the club jumpin' until six in the
morning. Hearing about benefit after benefit, cause after
cause, makes Rage seem like activist robots, and the question *Just who are these humorless mooks anyway?* starts to
form in your mind. In an interview with the *Chicago Tribune*, Tom acknowledged Rage is hardly Mötley Crüe II or
the second coming of 2 Live Crew but took pains to point
out that he believes all music is political and that his outfit
is just the extreme other side. "Some people ask us, 'Don't
you guys think you're kind of preachy and you're up on a
podium telling people what to do?' Well, everybody who's
up onstage, whether they like it or not, is being preachy
and on a podium telling people what to do. But for the
most part they're just telling them to kick back, just struggle
through that week and make it to the weekend and there's
going to be a couple of six-packs and maybe, if you have
the right acid-washed jeans, you'll get a girl as beautiful as
the ones in the beer commercials. That's basically what
consumer-culture desires are. We're the opposite side of
that coin."

And there are members of the band who occasionally

(gasp!) indulge in a little non-medical use of a certain green bud. You know, the wacky tobacky, ganja, dope, grass, the pot, Mary Jane, *la hierba, mota*. Shocking and scandalous as it may seem, in an interview with the pot smokers' chronicle *High Times*, Tim described his affection for the pungent weed. "I'm into it. I definitely get high. It's an innocent thing. Not everyone in the band blazes up, but Brad and I definitely partake in a little of the green herb so that we can be a tighter rhythm section. We're the tightest." And if that and the fact that Tom has a reputation for being the rock-band equivalent of a clubhouse cutup can't shake Rage's oh-so-serious image, then it may just be because to hear them tell it, the band isn't satisfied with a few benefit shows a year, or a whole catalog of songs detailing injustices all across the North American continent. In an interview with the *L.A. Times* Tom said the band goal is loftier still. "There are lots of bands who support some very noble causes, like abortion rights, environmental issues, and things like that. But we are talking about a bigger overhauling of society. To me, the reaction to our music is a reason for hope."

Oftentimes Rage's unapologetic politics earn them powerful enemies, people and organizations unaccustomed to being challenged by anyone, let alone a rock band from Los Angeles. The greatest example of this kind of high-powered resistance came when Rage Against the Machine organized a benefit for Mumia Abu-Jamal, a journalist on death row since his 1982 conviction for killing Daniel Faulkner, a Philadelphia cop. A former writer for National Public Radio, Mumia's presence on Death Row is a flashpoint issue given the ongoing controversy swirling around his trial. Supporters allege Mumia's conviction was a product of an inexperienced lawyer, a biased judge, witness tampering, and black jurors being kept off the jury. Others argue it's a clear-cut case of a cop killer on a fatal track to get what he deserves. The circumstances surrounding Faulkner's death are confusing but what is known is that he and Mumia's brother, William Cook, were engaged in an altercation after a traffic stop. Mumia happened to be in the area and when the dust settled, Faulkner lay dead, Mumia was wounded, and no one knew exactly what had brought the situation to bear. Some suggest the gun that killed Faulkner was of a different caliber than the one found in Mumia's possession, and others allege a third gunman did the killing. The fact that Mumia had organized the Philadelphia chapter of the Black Panther Party at age fifteen worked against him, as did his habit of using his weekly radio show as a forum to discuss instances of police brutality by the Philadelphia PD.

Tom outlined Rage's position in an interview with *Juice*. "The case of Mumia Abu-Jamal is a mainstream human-rights case. They try to paint it as something different, but everyone from Amnesty International to Archbishop Desmond Tutu, the European Parliament, to the Pennsylvania

Bar Association has said, 'You must not execute this guy because there are horrible discrepancies in this trial.' "

Mumia's attorney, Leonard Weinglass, took on the case in 1992, after being approached by Mumia's friends and family. Weinglass said that he became interested in the case and agreed to take it on after becoming better acquainted with the trial itself and the events that led up to it. "On the guilt/innocence issue there was the testimony of one prostitute that said she lied because she was threatened by police. There was a witness by the name of William Singletary who told police Mumia was not the shooter and they hounded him out of the city. There was another witness who we think did not come to testify, because she didn't want to help a black man, because she had been sexually abused by a black man. These were all witnesses who could have established his innocence who were not made available."

Rage learned about Mumia's plight when it became a free-speech issue. Jamal had recorded several segments about life in prison for NPR. The Fraternal Order of Police objected to some of the content and along with then Senate Majority Leader Bob Dole leaned on NPR to censor the broadcasts. Prison officials took punitive action after Mumia's book *Live from Death Row* was published. The public flap about these activities caught Rage's attention and they began to do their own research into his case. In a statement read at a press conference for the benefit Rage organized on Mumia's behalf, Zack explained how Rage got involved with his cause. "We found that Mr. Jamal was a prominent radio journalist in Philadelphia. He frequently reported cases of police misconduct on the air, and was threatened by then mayor Frank Rizzo. He had no criminal record but, as we later learned, he had an enormous FBI surveillance file they had kept on him since he was fifteen years old."

The weeks leading up to the January 28, 1999, benefit were tense. While Mumia had a virtual squadron of world leaders and human-rights organizations in his corner, he had the Fraternal Order of Police against him, who organized a boycott in an attempt to prevent Rage from hiring the ten off-duty officers needed for added security at the venue. Talk-radio host Howard Stern toed the law-and-order line on his top-ranked radio show, choosing to focus more on the idea that a cop had died and someone had to pay, than on whether or not Mumia pulled the trigger or had a fair chance to say he didn't in court. Stern also leaned on his employers at K-Rock to withdraw their support for the benefit show. Police officers began picketing outside Rage concerts in protest of the band's support of Mumia.

When New Jersey state officials learned that the concert, featuring Rage, the Beastie Boys, Black Star, and Bad Religion, was a benefit for an alleged murderer of a police officer, government officials objected. New Jersey governor Christine Todd Whitman expressed her opposition to the

Photo Credit: Steven Tackeff

Photo Credit: C. Radish

Photo Credit: C. Radish

Photo Credit: C. Radish

Photo Credit: C. Radish

Photo Credit: C. Radish

Photo Credit: C. Rac

show, along with state attorney general Peter Verniero and state police superintendent Carl Williams, and called for fans to return their tickets.

A week before the benefit, Faulkner's widow, Maureen Faulkner, had called New York's K-Rock radio station and talked about how distressed she was to learn that the fundraiser for Mumia's legal case was scheduled to take place. "I'm outraged. I heard about this about a week and a half ago off the Internet. I have a Web site and someone e-mailed me this, and I read it at ten o'clock at night and I was awake the entire night. I was just so upset that this band . . . They've been duped. In a way, I feel sorry for them because they have been misled by the defense attorney once again, and I would be willing to talk to them. I would be willing to give them the facts, the evidence, the court transcriptions that prove that Mumia received a fair trial and he is guilty of first-degree murder, of murdering my husband in cold blood."

Tom countered by calling the same radio station later in the day and reiterated Rage's reasons for playing the show. "In the United States of America you do not execute a man who did not have a fair trial. There's a word for that, and that word is 'lynching.' The Philadelphia Police Department has a long and glorious history of framing suspects. He is simply innocent of the crime."

Ever the vigilant activist, even as she navigates the upper reaches of her seventies, Mary Morello weighed in with her thoughts on the controversy in a guest editorial for *The*

Microphone: The Mass Mic Newsletter, volume 3, issue 1. "I do not understand the governor of New Jersey, who should be intelligent, Howard Stern, who may not be, and others who were implicated in condemning the concert! Is it too hard for them to believe that charges are sometimes trumped up, to at least have some kind of open mind when it comes to a person being guilty or not guilty, especially when there is evidence to the contrary?"

For a time CBS worked to arrange an on-air debate between Rage and the police to talk about the issues surrounding the case and the concert. In an interview with *Select* magazine, Tom claimed the debate was scrapped because the network feared the wrath of Rage fans. "The funny thing about that was how CBS wanted to set up a debate between us and the police. But they pulled out. It's not that they're afraid of us as a band, they're afraid of our audience. They know that when the facts of the case are drawn into the light, people are going to be pissed off! And they're going to want to do something about it."

The night of the show, activists turned up chanting, "Mumia is fearless! So are we! We won't stop until he's free!" and bands took time out to lead cheers of "Free Mumia!" or simply explained, as the Beastie Boys' Adam Yauch did, "It's not about us against them . . . it's about making it work for all of us."

Acknowledging the uproar that had preceded the concert, Zack addressed the crowd and reasserted why Rage chose to back Mumia's fight for a new trial. "Let me say straight up that tonight's benefit is not to support cop killers, or any other kind of killers. And if there were no question about the guilt of Mumia Abu-Jamal, we would not be holding this concert. We have a great deal of sympathy for anyone who is a victim of tragedy, including the widows of slain police officers. But we do not feel that the proper answer to tragedy is to inflict injustice on others. We need to base ourselves on fact, not emotion. Our path to closure should be paved with a search for truth and justice, not a search for revenge on whoever is targeted by police. It's ironic that tonight, on the day that the Pope called for an end to the death penalty in the United States, we have others outside calling for the taking of a life on the flimsiest of evidence.

"Rasta rebel, the revered Bob Marley sings, 'Get up, stand up. Stand up for your rights.' It is in just such a spirit that I salute those who have not yet bent their will nor surrendered their rights to the state; they want to read what they want to read, say what they want to say, and support what they want to support."

Cops picketed the benefit concert and encouraged the concert-goers to ask for refunds rather than attend the show. In an interview with the English music magazine *New Musical Express*, Tom explained Rage's tribute to the cops who would have blocked them from playing if given the chance.

"The police hounded us through our entire U.S. tour.

They called for a boycott of Rage albums and Rage shows, and they absolutely failed. I don't know if this joke means anything in England, but in the U.S., the police spend a lot of time in doughnut shops drinking coffee. We sent them out three hundred doughnuts, courtesy of the band. We figured if they weren't out there protecting the community, they might at least be well fed."

Causing controversy and stirring the pot can make already-complicated things like touring harder, but Brad said, in an interview with the Australian Web site *the I* that Rage's brand of rabble-rousing and muckraking rock are essential as the counterpoint to the mostly vapid rock scene in America. "Especially in the U.S., there needs to be a band like this. If you look at how many bands are singing about getting drunk and having a good time — and I'm not saying that I never get drunk and have a good time. But the ratio of those bands compared to bands that are actually saying something — with full credit to Zack and what he's doing — it's kinda astronomical. When you're talking about the things we're talking about, you're gonna piss people off, and you are gonna get people who wanna slander you in the press. And that's fine, because when you have opinions like ours it's gonna happen."

Skeptics argue that fans are just there to rock out. Sure they might grab a flyer at the show and join in a chant like "Police suck," but those kids go home and wake up the next day, throw out the flyer, and talk about how drunk they got and how many way hot chicks were there, right?

That's all the kids care about. Booze and a little eye-candy. Leonard Weinglass, Mumia's attorney, sees the situation a little differently. "It certainly has had an impact on a significant segment of the youth population. The concert for Mumia at the Meadowlands was the single largest event in which his case was put forward, larger than any of the street demonstrations in San Francisco, Philadelphia, and New York. Having his name prominently mentioned in the CDs and getting the kids wearing his T-shirts really has put his case before the youth of this country. I do a lot of speaking at universities and very often students will say to me the first time they heard of Mumia was through Rage. They were very curious and that's why they came to see me speak.... There's no other spokepeople for Mumia reaching people in the tens of thousands except for Rage."

Although Rage's politics always register somewhere far left of the dial, by supporting Mumia they ran the risk of alienating the type of fan who bought the records, bobbed their head to the heavy beats, and never gave the lyrics much thought. Thousands of fans bought tickets to the Mumia benefit, but when the state of New Jersey took great pains to spell out exactly where the money raised from the concert would go, a certain percentage did ask for refunds.

Jim Kerr, alternative-music editor of the trade publication *Radio & Records*, said that kind of backlash is a risk built into what Rage does as a band, where political opinions come part and parcel with their songs. "I think that's always a risk you take when you make a political stand.

The risk you take is that your stance will not just be the opposite of the opinion of the majority, but so far outside of it that [the fans] lose the respect they had for [the band]. Whenever you're in a band that takes a firm stand on a politically sensitive issue, you have to take it for granted you're going to piss some people off. I thought they were going to get in a lot more hot water for the Mumia benefit than they did."

Beastie Boy Adam Yauch laid partial blame on the media for the furor surrounding the concert, claiming they failed to fully explain the issues at stake in an interview with MTV. "I think there was a lot of misinformation in the press around the concert. I think that a lot of people didn't even really know [what it was about]. There were people on the radio saying, 'Oh, it's a concert being held for a cop killer.' So I think a lot of people heard that first bit of information and didn't find out more about what was actually being put forward."

In the weeks after the concert, Zack followed up the benefit by flying to Switzerland and making an appearance before the United Nations' Commission on Human Rights in Geneva, outlining the problems and issues with Mumia's first trial and requesting they put pressure on the U.S. government to grant a new trial for Mumia.

In 1996 the Beastie Boys worked with the Milarepa Fund in coordinating the first Tibetan Freedom Concert, in Golden Gate Park in San Francisco. Part of a lineup that included the Foo Fighters, Smashing Pumpkins, Beck, A Tribe Called Quest, Fugees, Yoko Ono, and the Red Hot Chili Peppers, Rage played on June 16, the second day of the two-day festival, rendering a set that included "Freedom," "Killing in the Name," and "Vietnow." In an interview with the Associated Press, Yoko Ono explained why she thought the concert was such an important one. "Freedom and peace are important for not just Tibet but for our homeland, our planet, and that's what we're working on. This is the starting point, and when we do this and feel the togetherness and the energy and the power of togetherness, then probably there is a chain reaction to that."

The crowd went particularly bonkers during Rage's frenetic set and before day's end the band had won themselves an unlikely fan. San Francisco mayor Willie Brown proclaimed his love for Rage, as they tore through "Killing in the Name." "I love them! I love the spirit, and I love the energy — I think it's just beautiful. I mean," he said, in reference to the thousands of fans moshing about, "do you see that scene out there?"

Mike D of the festival-organizing Beastie Boys seconded Da Mayor's vote for Rage's live show in the same article. "The main thing with Rage Against the Machine is that when it comes to rocking a crowd, no way you can beat them."

Rage also signed on for the 1999 edition of the Tibetan Freedom Concert. Initially slated to play the Amsterdam show, organizers bumped Rage to the Chicago stage in an effort to boost ticket sales for the gig. Joining a lineup that included the Beastie Boys, Biz Markie, Līve, Outkast, and the Cult was a no-brainer for a band so caught up in causes. In an interview with Rollingstone.com, Tom talked about why playing the Tibetan Freedom Concert was a priority. "We're playing this show because we oppose oppression in all its forms. In Tibet now, injustices and violence are perpetrated against people of that region. But what's sometimes forgotten is that prior to the communist takeover, there were also injustices and violence perpetrated against people, particularly women and the lower classes. It was basically was a feudal society. What I think everyone here at the concert wants is self-determination, justice, and equality for all the people of Tibet."

Given the fact that Rage releases a record about as often as we elect a president, it's understandable that die-hard fans have learned to look forward to the multitude of side projects, singles, and soundtrack work the band members do while waiting for their volatile chemistry to find its level again.

This pattern held up during the lull between *Evil Empire* and *The Battle of Los Angeles* with the release of "No Shelter," which was released as part of the blockbuster *Godzilla* soundtrack. Critics of Rage pointed to the placement of "No Shelter" in one of the biggest summer movies of 1998 and claimed it reeked of selling out or hopping in bed with the enemy. Tom defended the band's decision in an interview with *Kerrang!* "A lot of times a soundtrack is an opportunity to collaborate with musicians you admire. It's an opportunity to work outside of your band, or exercise—you know, to flex your musical abilities when Rage has downtime. Out of *Godzilla*, we happened to get a great song in 'No Shelter.'"

Rage's cover of Bruce Springsteen's "The Ghost of Tom Joad" missed the cut for Rage's records but popped up on their 1997 collection of videos. Although many fans immediately think of Springsteen's headbanded, fist-pumping, arena glory days, ideologically, Rage and Jersey Bruce enjoy a great deal of overlap when it comes to the issues at the root of their songs. Tom admitted that during his metalhead days he would heckle pals who shelled out hard-earned cash to watch The Boss, in an interview with Guitar.com. "I'd say, 'Are you out of your mind? All that money and he's not even heavy metal?' And I went through an anti-Bruce phase when *Born in the U.S.A.* was popular, because I hadn't really listened to the words and there were some songs that were really syrupy-sweet. . . . But then he was on HBO or something doing an Amnesty International concert from Brazil, and I couldn't believe what I saw. It was so moving."

Tom said hearing "The Ghost of Tom Joad" for the first time had a similar effect, and described his first listen of the tune and Rage's subsequent update of it, in an interview with *Addicted to Noise*. "When I got that record and first put ['Tom Joad'] on, it was the most compelling since

Jane's Addiction's 'Nothing Shocking.' The lyrical message of that song of redemption through struggle fits very comfortably with the Rage Against the Machine catalog. We gave it a brand-new musical base. It's been sort of a staple of our set, and I'm sure will continue to be. It's something we're really proud of."

During the collaboration for "Snoop Bounce" that paired Tom and Brad with rapper Snoop Dogg for the benefit album *Music for our Mother Ocean: Volume 3*, Brad picked up an idea to enhance his drumming from watching Snoop bob to the tune. "If you watch him when he's listening to a song, his head is going up on the '1'," Brad told *Drum!* "And if you look at, like, Beavis and Butthead, their heads are going down on the '1.' What I tried to do was to take the essence of those hip-hop, laid-back verses, and then taking what I was talking about—the spirit of Keith Moon—and actually leave out a half of a beat."

The laundry list of Tom's side work includes recording Pink Floyd's "Another Brick in the Wall" in a supergroup with Stephen Perkins (Jane's Addiction) and Layne Staley (Alice in Chains), but to date he lists his favorite project as a collaboration between himself and Prodigy. In an interview with *Kerrang!* Tom talked about hearing Prodigy mastermind Liam Howlett assimilate Tom's guitar-playing into the driving force of an electronica track. "I'd love to work with them again. I think that in Liam Howlett's work there is a brilliance to the songwriting, the arranging, and the production work which is really unique, and meshes very, very well with my guitar-playing and pushes it in different directions."

Howlett also praised the collaboration, and in an interview with *Addicted to Noise* asserted he would have liked a little more time to work on it. "It's just like Tom and me grooving on this track. He's very experimental. He's got some scratchy stuff he does with a guitar and it's quite a slow groove. It was written for the film. It's nothing too complicated. I literally had about four days so it was kind of rushed. I was happy with the results but I wish I had another week on it to really sculpture it. Yeah, it sounds good. I'm happy with it."

As Primus readied themselves to enter the studio to record 1999's "Anti-Pop," Les Claypool and crew decided to forgo working with conventional producers and instead put together a wish list of musicians to produce the album. Tom got tapped to step behind the boards, along with Tom Waits, Stewart Copeland, former drummer for the Police, and Fred Durst of Limp Bizkit. In addition to his production work on "Electric Uncle Sam," "Mama Didn't Raise No Fool," and "Power Mad," Tom co-wrote the three songs, something Les Claypool told bassguitar.com has rarely happened with the over one hundred songs penned by Primus. "Tom Morello was the first person we worked with; we recorded the tracks for his three songs in three days, and then we did the vocals up here. He co-wrote those songs; all three started with his riffs. He is the only person who's ever come into the Primus world and caused me to just hand over the reins and sit back. He definitely called the shots the whole way, like it was his band all three days. And it was *awesome*. At no point did I go, 'I don't know, dude'—I felt so comfortable."

Outside of the "Snoop Bounce," Brad's side work has been confined to as-of-yet-unsurfaced recording and jam sessions with everyone from his girlfriend and former Seven-Year Bitch singer Selene Vigil, to Cypress Hill and former Circle Jerks guitarist Zander Schloss. In an interview with *Rip It Up*, Brad raved about playing with Schloss. "He's an amazing guitar player. Me and him will get together on an afternoon, not say a word for a couple of hours and just communicate through music. The freedom is incredible; I mean, the amount of telepathy that goes on is just awesome. It's free-form jamming that I enjoy tremendously. I also try to run every day or every other day, to keep my mind and body in tune. I'm also pretty good at the whole Taoist Zen thing of not doing anything. I also ride motorcycles quite a bit. I enjoy that a lot."

Zack's extracurricular activities revolve around his stints volunteering in Chiapas, and the Spitfire Tour. Featuring spoken-word performances and speeches from the likes of former Dead Kennedys singer Jello Biafra, former Nirvana bassist Krist Novoselic, the Indigo Girls' Amy Ray, and actor Woody Harrelson, Zack helped conceive the Spitfire Tour as a means of addressing issues ranging from homophobia to medical marijuana. With most venues set on college campuses, the Spitfire Tour offered an opportunity for kids to get information about a variety of issues from artists whose work they respect. Sarah Haines of On Board Entertainment said Zack's extensive phonebook helped get the tour off the ground in 1998, giving organizers the numbers they needed to get the ball rolling. "When we wanted to get in touch with Amy Ray from the Indigo Girls, Zach knew her and approached her for us. He's helped us get to people we couldn't get to on our own—since of course he had their home phone numbers."

The video collection *Rage Against the Machine* helped bridge the gap between albums. It featured live and uncensored versions of songs such as "People of the Sun" and "Killing in the Name." The most noteworthy clips came from the 1994 Pink Pop festival in Holland. Playing to a frenzied throng in excess of one hundred thousand, Rage ignited the audience to the extent that the force of their excitement registered on the Richter scale. In an interview with *Addicted to Noise* Tom talked about the explosive gig. "[There were amazing scenes from] the Holland show, the ones of 'Freedom' and 'Killing in the Name' from the Pink Pop festival. The lead story from the *Holland Daily News* the next day was that the crowd, during our set, literally registered on the Richter scale at 1.1. [There was] a little graph and the time frames. Like, Rage's set starts and then it kinda spikes up. It was pretty amazing."

On January 21, 1997, a day when Democrats gathered in Washington, D.C., to clap each other on the back and

ring in President Bill Clinton's second term in the Oval
Office, Rage Against the Machine gathered in an L.A. studio to hold an anti-Inaugural assembly of sorts. Billed as
Radio Free L.A., Rage took the opportunity to get live music on the air from Cypress Hill, Beck, the Indigo Girls,
bassist Flea from the Red Hot Chili Peppers, and drummer
Stephen Perkins of Jane's Addiction. Beamed out by sat-
ellite and Internet radio, the broadcast also featured on-air
interviews with Chuck D, Zapatista Subcommandante
Marcos, Mumia Abu-Jamal, and Leonard Peltier.

"They used to come to the shows in Atlanta at a time
when I was having a lot of difficulty lining up bands for
the Radio Free L.A. show," Morello told *MTV News* about
the Indigo Girls' appearance on Radio Free L.A. and his
subsequent remixing of their song "Shed My Skin." "They
volunteered to participate and I thought that was really
cool, and I think from an ideological standpoint we're kind
of on the same footing, so I was happy to do it. And it gave
me the opportunity to play drums and bass and guitar on
a track, and human beatbox on a track, which was really
interesting."

For all of Rage's outspoken politicism, the band feels
little affiliation with the two major parties of our time, seek-
ing to throw their hat in a more radical ring. The Radio
Free L.A. broadcast was as much a reminder that the far
left exists and is populated with people eager for change,
as it was entertainment. In an interview with *Vox*, Zack

expounded on his political philosophy. "I see very little difference between the two parties. They eat from the same trough, they serve the same purpose. . . . There is very little difference between a liberal and conservative capitalist. I have no faith, nor do I align myself with, nor do I recognize the legitimacy of the current political system. What I have seen, by being involved with the communities, is a much more empowered and enraged student movement, one which aligns itself with the struggles of janitors and of indigenous communities in southeast Mexico."

"Obviously the show was filled with plenty of messages," Morello told MTV News. "I think that it's appropriate to have a rebuttal to all the glad-handing and smiling and 'Oh, it's gonna be another great four years.' For a lot of people it's not going to be a great four years, just like the last years wasn't a great four years. And so those are some of the stories we wanted to tell tonight. And while there's a lot of celebration, a lot of joy that happened in the music tonight, there's a serious content as well."

Rage also used the off-time between records to work on individual causes. Using the clout of the Rage name, band members were able to direct attention to issues and protests that might have gone unnoticed otherwise. Concerned that members of the Garment Workers United Union were being forced to work in sweatshop conditions, Tom attended a protest on their behalf in Santa Monica, California, and ended up getting arrested. Tom told Addicted to Noise that

his involvement in the march was something of a calcu-
lated gamble. "We're against it because they use sweatshop
labor in Calcutta or whatever, and in the United States—in
Los Angeles, New York City, and the Bay Area. They have,
like, slave-labor conditions. And they're counting on the
people that are reading this not to care. And they think
that fashion is more important and whatever, and so the
brutal exploitation of those workers isn't going to matter to
them. We're betting that they're wrong." In addition to
marching in the protest, advertisements were commis-
sioned the same week that ran in Las Vegas and New York
featuring a band photo and a caption reading, "Rage
Against Sweatshops: We Don't Wear Guess?®—A Message
from Rage Against the Machine and UNITE." Timed to
coincide with the Christmas season, Rage hoped to dis-
courage Rage fans who might also be Guess?® consumers
from buying Guess?® products during the biggest shopping
season of the year. Tom explained that the overlap between
Rage's audience and Guess?®-wearing kids caused the
band to single out Guess?® in an interview with *Addicted
to Noise*. "I think it's less a matter of personal preference
and more that that's one of the more glaring issues facing
us and one that our audience can relate to. The demographic that is targeted by the clothing manufacturers who
employ sweatshop labor is the same demographic that buys
Rage Against the Machine records." In an era when rock
bands are increasingly comfortable and well paid for shil-
ling for companies, Rage's anti-Guess?® stance struck a par-

ticularly jarring chord, and certainly captured the attention of the Guess?® company.

In the spring of 1997, Rage signed on to be the opening act for the first two weeks of U2's over-the-top Pop Mart tour/extravaganza, with Rage's net profits donated to such activist and free-speech organizations as the Zapatista Front for National Liberation, Friends and Family of Mumia Abu-Jamal, Women Alive, UNITE (garment workers' union), and FAIR (Fairness and Accuracy in Reporting). Although U2's elaborate production on the Pop Mart tour might have seemed at odds with Rage's spartan political stance, Tom said in an MTV interview he became a fan of U2 while stuck working a crummy day job in L.A. after he graduated from Harvard. "I was a filing clerk. I alphabetized eight hours a day, all by myself, and the bosses were very cruel, and I was superpoor making sub-minimum wage doing this. And I had one tape, and it was the *Unforgettable Fire*, and it was listening to that, hours and hours, day after day, month after month that helped me get through that time . . . because in that music there's so much hope and so much passion that really helped me transcend that mundane, you know, grim, crappy experience and I've been a fan ever since."

The Woodstock name comes with a cachet unmatched by most festivals. In the summer of 1999 promoters lined up a glittering galaxy of rock stars that included Korn, Limp Bizkit, Metallica, Jewel, DMX, Alanis Morissette, Dave Matthews Band, Red Hot Chili Peppers, and Sheryl Crow to make the trek north to Rome, New York, for the three-day festival. Scheduled for July 23–25, the festival came at the peak of summer's strength. Instead of the peace-and-love fest the graybeards yammer on about, Woodstock '99 would be remembered as a violent fiasco. Lingering images of the 1999 festival center around fans burning and looting, while media coverage zeroed in on the rapes alleged to have occurred in the mosh pits and the lack of water and clean facilities available to the several hundred thousand festival-goers.

Almost lost in all the hoopla was the fact that Rage played their first set in some time at Woodstock '99. Sandwiched between Limp Bizkit and Metallica, the festival had begun to veer out of control long before Rage took the stage. Although Zack usually utilizes the limelight as a chance to address crowds directly, he said little during the show aside from an introduction of "It's been over twenty years, there's no proof, and he's still in jail," a thinly veiled reference to Leonard Peltier's incarceration, for "Freedom." Rage did give the thirsty horde a preview of the record to come, playing "Broken Man" to a crowd mostly hearing the song for the first time. Tim, at this point going by his latest moniker Y Tim K, punctuated the proceedings by torching the U.S. flag from the stage. In an interview with *Rolling Stone*, Tim explained the reasoning that led him to burn Old Glory before an audience of nearly a quarter million people. "The flag represents all my freedoms — one of them is my right to express myself. My burning the flag is as much glorifying as desecrating it."

For Brad, playing Woodstock was a completely disheartening gig. Seeing fans attack the barriers and light standards and hearing bands screaming about wanting to "break stuff," left a bad taste in his mouth. In an interview with the Australian publication *The Age*, Brad reflected on his feelings about playing Woodstock. "I want to remember what happened, but maybe I just blocked it out because it was such a horrible experience. But when we went on, I remember feeling disenchanted with the whole situation. We just played and left, and thought, 'That was just fucked'; rather than try to preach to a bunch of people who had just rioted, we just played the show, stuck to our message, hoped for the best and split. I don't know, but that's what we did. It was wack."

Coverage of Woodstock bordered on the hysterical. Web sites filed multiple reports each hour, updating situations that no one had a handle on yet. Television stations replayed the same stock photos of bonfires and tipped cars often enough to where a casual observer might have mistaken the troubled scene for footage of a war-torn area, instead of what it was, the ragged end of a weekend gone horribly wrong.

In a scathing editorial that ran in the *New York Times*, Tom lashed out at the media for paying more attention to the fires and toppled towers at Woodstock, than to issues of global concern. "Indignant editorials and television broadcasts raving over the 'horrific violence' and 'terrifying blazes' were rampant. But, when U.S. Tomahawk missiles lit a children's hospital outside of Belgrade on fire, killing many inside, it was not chewed over to this extent. More incredulous attention was paid to kids' setting fires at Woodstock."

Other targets of Tom's wrath in the editorial included the festival promoters whom he claimed jacked up the price of water in an attempt to squeeze more profits out of the event, and the criminal actions of those who committed sexual assaults as the concert was in progress. "Yes, Woodstock was filled with predators: the degenerate idiots who assaulted those women, the greedy promoters who wrung every cent out of thirsty concertgoers, and last but not least, the predator media that turned a blind eye to real violence and scapegoated the quarter of a million music fans at Woodstock '99, the vast majority of whom had the time of their lives."

When Brad heard the extent of the mayhem, he compared his reaction to Charlie Watts's take when Watts learned of the killings at Altamont. "I really regret playing Woodstock. If I could do things again, that's the one show out of my whole career I could say that I wish we hadn't done. I felt just like Charlie when I found out what had happened. 'Oh, no! Festival gone wrong.'"

We realized that if we were a little more subtle, if we
branched out a little, we might reach more people. We
finally saw that we had just been reaching the same people
over and over. And the music—just *bang, bang, bang*—was
getting to be like a nagging wife. This way if kids hear the
record, then maybe they'll start humming the songs. And if
they start humming the songs maybe they'll read the lyrics
and get something from them.
　　　　　　—Mick Jones of the Clash, *Rolling Stone*

Truly great songs sneak up on you, jump you, throw you
to the ground, stand looming over you, and demand
you listen. They might seem inconspicuous or sugar-pop
sweet at first, but sooner or later the candy coating wears
off and you start digesting its full meaning and scope. On
the first two Rage records the digestion process wasn't a
long one. You knew what you had. You had Zack screaming, Tom's taut riffs, and Brad and Tim, the rhythm section
in lockstep. It didn't take long to dissect what Zack was
trying to get at with songs like "Freedom" and "Killing in
the Name." With the new record came new sounds. Some
critics had lambasted Rage in the past for falling into the
"all the songs sound the same" rut, with the same abrasive
groove each time and not once pausing to reload. Other

artists challenged Rage, claiming they weren't taking enough chances. In an interview with the *Boston Globe*, Trent Reznor of Nine Inch Nails damned Rage with faint praise and essentially suggested they'd found their corner of the market and were timidly cowering in it. "I can't think of anything in rock that has excited me lately," he added. "The bands that are somewhat exciting seem to be themselves. I'd say Rage Against the Machine is an example of that. They're a really good band, playing it safe and repeating, but they keep writing the same song. I hold them in high regard, but I don't hear anything that's really making people think."

In the years since Rage last made a record the musical climate had changed. When *Evil Empire* came out, grunge was still something besides what accumulates on the timing chain in your car, and the dawning of the brief ska and swing revivals was nigh. Four years later and swing and ska had had their flings and bubblegum pop was dominating the landscape, along with a whole host of bands playing the same fused style of rap and rock Rage had perfected in the early 1990s. Instead of moaning about the new bands copping their style, in an interview with *Rock Sound* Tom acknowledged that borrowing ideas and styles is an essential part of being a musician, something he himself has done. "Well, when we came out in '91 there was no one like us, but of course there's a whole genre now of rock/rap bands. A lot of the hard-rock part of Rage comes from Led Zeppelin or Black Sabbath, whereas newer bands draw more on Metallica or Pantera. I can't criticize bands for maybe stealing our sound. I mean, we've got influences too. I would hate Tony Iommi [Black Sabbath] or Terminator X [Public Enemy] to hold a grudge because Rage Against the Machine are guilty of a liberal borrowing of some of their sounds."

With the arrival of so-called "Adidas rock" as a genre, there was an unspoken pressure on Rage as the elder statesmen of the style to make a record that would put the young bucks in their place and show that the mean old dogs still had it in 'em. In the year before the album's release band members were coy about what kind of musical stew they were simmering. Vague quotes about it being the funkiest and most groove-laden record yet, leaked out with metronomic regularity. *Tick*, this record's got some of the deepest funk we've come up with yet, *tock*, the grooves on this record are unbeatable, *tick*, this may just be our best record ever. And so on. In an interview with *Guitar World* Tom talked about "Sleep Now in the Fire" in its formative stages, shedding some light on what had been some very gray areas.

"The working title for this song was 'MC5' because it has the raw feel of the Stooges or the MC5 mixed with Rage's thunderous rhythm section. I couldn't help but envision a huge festival audience jumping up and down to this one—it has that kind of feel. The song really took shape when we married the main guitar riff to a very seventies, rolling bass line with a dark, lava-lamp, incense-burning, groovy vibe. It reminds me a little of a group from the early seventies called the Jimmy Castor Bunch. Big Afros. Big bass lines. Timmy and Brad really swing this groove."

Once again paired with producer Brendan O'Brien, who was behind the boards for *Evil Empire*, Rage had picked O'Brien in part for the relaxed atmosphere he creates in the studio, a crucial quality for a band whose past recording sessions had been sometimes notoriously tense. Having witnessed some of the lower points of the band going into *The Battle of Los Angeles*, O'Brien was now familiar with his self-described role as "umpire" for band disputes and deliberately set a relaxed tone. "Making the last record was just not a lot of fun," O'Brien told *Alternative Press*. "There were too many outside forces that were making it much more difficult. But I think the band sees things a lot more eye-to-eye now, and I was trying to get as much out of that as I could."

Tom described the mood in an O'Brien-run recording session to *Alternative Press*. "We're spoiled with Brendan because with a lot of [other producers] it sounds like [they make recording] a lot of hard work. But it's actually fun to make a record with him. We choose microphones by color coordination! It's like, 'Oh that red mike looks really good with the Che [Guevara flag] on your amp. We'll go with that one!' "

Early rehearsals yielded immediate results. With the new

songs still in skeletal form, Rage tried to picture playing the tunes to a live audience. In an article in *Spin*, Tom talked about the band's reaction to songs that were starting to take shape. "It was thrilling to go into our little Hollywood rehearsal studio every day—the funk was deep, the rock was heavy. When we'd hear what would later become the chorus [of the first single] 'Guerilla Radio' or the intro to 'Sleep Now in the Fire,' we would just close our eyes and picture sixty thousand people jumping up and down. Just going off."

Lessons learned from the pressure cooker in Atlanta, Rage made sure to leave time for things less intense than the process of writing thoughtful and tuneful rock songs. Y Tim K described the downtime in an interview with *Alternative Press*. "It went smoothly because we didn't let ourselves burn out. We took time out every day to just chill or play touch football outside the studio. We'd videotape it and then watch it in slow motion—it was so perfect. It was the hardest I'd laughed in years."

In an interview with *Addicted to Noise*, Tom insisted that the touch-football sessions were not abnormal for the band and they were not the boring drones they are sometimes made out to be. "When we're playing our songs, whether it's in the studio or whether it's onstage, we take it dead seriously. But as far as the lives of the band members 24-7, there's probably more frivolity than you might guess . . . certainly more touch football than they guess."

*   *   *

During the tour for *Evil Empire* Rage got in the habit of jamming and writing a song onstage each night. Back in off the road, they kept jamming, and with the recording equipment on standby, managed to corral some happy accidents into songs. " 'Mic Check' was a song that came out of that kind of vibe; we were taking five, and Zack got on the drum kit and came up with a beat, and Timmy had a bunch of new, interesting wah-wah pedals and distortion things he started making noise through," Tom told *Wall of Sound*. "That's kind of similar in a way to how 'People of the Sun' came together: We just started playing through it, and it fell together in a hurry."

Jamming sparked many of the parts to the new songs, and keeping an open ear for happenstance played a role as well. In his column for *Guitar World* Tom described how the radio bit at the end of "Sleep Now in the Fire" worked its way onto the album. "I found that when I turned on the pedal but didn't play anything, I picked up a crystal-clear signal from a Korean radio station. In earlier mixes of 'Sleep Now in the Fire,' that radio thing was featured more prominently. We had the radio signal running through the entire song. It was a little annoying, so we decided just to stick it at the very end. I always like to say that there are no samples on any of our records, and this is a good example. That radio signal is no sample—it was played!

"Our last day at A&M Studios was October 1 of '98, and

the music has changed some since then, as the lyrics came together; we did some editing or lengthening of verses. But I think the final vocals were probably finished right after we played Woodstock [in July]. So it went right up to the eleventh hour with the mastering to make our release date."

While doing some production work on Primus's *Anti-Pop* album, Tom gave bassist Les Claypool a sneak preview of "Calm Like a Bomb" and seeing his jaw drop made Tom realize he was on the right track. "I actually played the instrumental version of that song for Les Claypool a few months before the record was done, and he was just like, 'What are you guys doing? Like, what the hell is going on?' If Les Claypool is scratching his head, then you know you're on the right track," Tom said in an interview with MTV. "That's just a really heavy song . . . and I think that song has some of Zack's best lyrics he's ever written."

Rage's glacial pace in recording albums partially stemmed from Zack's perfectionist bent. The music for *The Battle of Los Angeles* was completed nearly a year before the record's release. Knowing his need to work in this way, the rest of the group recorded their parts to improvised lyrics which then get thrust under Zack's microscope for intense scrutiny and revision. In an interview with *Addicted to Noise*, Tom talked about recording without set lyrics. "He's freestyling the lyrics, so you know which parts are gonna be rapping, which parts are gonna be ferocious, which parts are gonna be whispered. So you can tailor and

and arrange the song to the vocals, even though there might not be a final lyric sheet. As far as the actual words on the page, often they bear little resemblance to the final product."

Some of the delay comes from the natural ebb and flow of creativity. Granted, most bands' tides come in a lot more often than Rage's but in an interview with *Rolling Stone* Brad suggested that the lengthy gap between albums plays a significant role in keeping the band together. "The energy between us is not an even-keeled thing. Either nothing's going on or we're 110 percent full-on. Maybe that is the reason we still are able to do this. We take the time off before we get sick of each other and break up."

Rage finished up recording at A&M Studios in October of 1998 and though the music changed some, much of the time between then and the November 1999 release of the record had passed with Zack working on his lyrics and subsequently recording his vocal parts.

The musical portion of the album finished, Tim took advantage of the time to come up with his latest moniker. Having already cruised through Timmy C, Tim Bob, and his personal favorite Simmerin' T, he cast his name changing eyes toward the millennium, and settled on Y Tim K. In an interview with Launch.com, Tim explained the frequent changes in his nom de guerre. "It's just fun. At the start, there was this part of me that was like, 'I don't want people to know who I am.' And I do live an anonymous lifestyle. I go home from tours and making records and live anonymously. I don't have to field questions all the time about Rage Against the Machine, and I like that. It's nice to be able to walk onstage and be a rock star for a little while, and then go back home and be a homeowner [*laughs*]. I thought [Y Tim K] was the best name I've come up with in a while. My last name, though, Simmerin' T, was what I was called on the *Godzilla* soundtrack, for 'No Shelter.' I was really into that name, but it never got the props that it deserved. Simmerin' T was definitely good."

As the rest of the band sat on their hands and bit their tongues, Zack labored to create lyrics he felt were up to par. His disdain for much of the current commercially-popular hip-hop fueled his desire to write words that did a little more than get the booties moving in clubs. In an interview with *George* magazine, Zack offered a dim assessment of the state of hip-hop's top acts. "It's just this fabrication. It's a shame the way most popular hip-hop is so devoid of real commentary. I look at Puff Daddy or Jay-Z and I think, 'Fuck, man, if Ronald Reagan was a rapper, he'd be in Puff Daddy's crew.' The materialism and indi-viduality—'I'm taking mine'—it's Reaganism." Inspired as always by the militant politicism of words by Chuck D and Joe Strummer, Zack also allowed influences as far-flung as Cuban poet Jose Marti, musician/poet Gil Scott-Heron, and Uruguayan journalist Eduardo Galeano to seep into his work. In an interview with *Rolling Stone*, Zack admitted he's not the world's fastest worker and attributed some of the delay to a desire to change his lyrical writing style. "I have the Leonard Cohen approach to writing. You start a great piece—and six or seven months down the line, you pick it up again and work with it. I have to make sure this music resonates with people, that it doesn't talk to them. What I did a lot on the last record was, 'This is what I think. This is my comment.' I've had to change. I want people to see reflections of themselves in the songs."

As a means of moving in that direction, Zack penned some his most personal lyrics to date, delving into some of the difficulties he had experienced after Beto suffered his mental breakdown. The frustration he felt watching his father go from being a hugely talented artist to an obsessive religious fanatic who had forced a young and growing Zack to fast, surfaced in "Born of a Broken Man." Lines like "raped the spirit he was supposed to nurture," allude to Beto's quitting his art and destroying his work. Tim's known Zack the longest, and told *Spin* that hearing Zack sing those lines has brought the band closer together. "I know how hard those words are for Zack to sing. They represent so much pain. But the fact that he put that out there makes me feel like we're more of a band."

Zack's patience paid off as critics and bandmates alike responded to his seamless flow and pointed commentary. In an interview with the *Album Network* Tom commented on Zack's vocal work on the new record. "I think that Zack does a phenomenal job on this record. He has completely hit the nail on the head in combining the politics and the poetry, then synthesizing that into great rhymes. And that's not an easy task. His peers as a vocalist are other rappers, as opposed to other guys in rock bands who sometimes rap; I think that's more clear than ever on this record."

Rolling Stone awarded the new record four stars and noted the shift in style, saying, "The record starts off with the explosion that Rage Against the Machine have always wanted to drop: The first three songs ('Testify,' 'Guerrilla Radio,' 'Calm Like a Bomb') are near-perfect fusions of spit and fury. Hell, 'Guerrilla Radio' even has a harmonica solo you can bang your head to. This is adrenaline-pumping rock and roll first, political agenda second." Mary Poppins might have been on to something with her "spoonful of sugar" theory. A band pal and rap star in his own right, Chuck D of Public Enemy gave Zack's lyrics props in an interview with *Addicted to Noise* and offered high praise, saying Rage's work reminded him of P.E.'s efforts over a decade ago.

"When Public Enemy came out with a nationalistic point of view it was unprecedented in pop music to rage against the machine. We raged against the machine and motherfuckers were like, 'How dare you be a slave and rebel against the hand that . . . ?' Not only did we bite the hand that fed us, we tried to chop it off. That set a precedent for a lot of the artists to come out and do their particular thing. Zack is pushing the envelope."

Yet no one has succeeded in combining such aggressive, cathartic music with the relevant, inspiring words that have become Rage's signature. In fact, just as the genre is about to dissolve into a mass of jockstrap-grabbing nonsense, Tom Morello and company return with a set that valiantly aims to focus America's anger-afflicted youth toward more politically aware topics. Loyalists will be struck by how Rage's typically high degree of intensity seems to have exploded off the meter. Cuts like "Testify" and the first single, "Guerrilla Radio," resonate like a riotous battle cry of righteous revolution.

Prolific by nature, Tom admitted to *Wall of Sound* that if he had his druthers Rage would make records more than once an Olympiad, but also offered some perspective on the time that passes between albums. "It's a chemistry that does not always work at a sprinter's pace, and that's okay. I've come to accept that. I've played with dozens of other people, some of the best musicians around, in different musical situations, to keep my chops up and for fun. But it's nothing that approximates what it's like to play with Zack and Timmy and Brad. And if I have to wait a little longer to make records with those guys, that's all right. It's worth the wait."

With headquarters in Los Angeles, the title *The Battle of Los Angeles*, for Rage, reflected the band's diversity and that of Los Angeles at large, as well as the growing gap between the wealthy *haves* in their Beverly Hills homes, and the Dumpster-diving have-nots struggling to survive, and everyone in between. In an interview with the *Toronto Sun*, Tom talked about the title of the new record. "The front that L.A. puts on to the world is that of Hollywood and glamour, unbelievable wealth and power. Bubbling not far from the surface are tremendous divisions of race and class, tremendous amounts of volatility. Those occasionally spill over into insurrection."

Bringing Rage's music and message to all points of the globe began as, and remains, a goal of the band. On October 30, 1999, just a few days before *The Battle of Los Angeles* would see the light of day, the band took another step in that direction, with a gig at the East Pavilion of the Sorts Palace in Mexico City, Mexico. Rage's outspoken stance on the Zapatistas' situation in Chiapas meant the band's arrival in Mexico City would pack a powerful punch. With their fingers on the pulse of the political unrest prevalent in the area, their show before five thousand delirious fans carried a political significance absent in most rock concerts. Pancho Paredes, drummer for Maldita Vecindad and a writer for the liberal daily *Reforma*, commented on what Rage coming to Mexico meant to the people there, in an interview with *Spin* magazine. "Put it this way, there are two ways of being modern, and the one to the south of the Rio Grande usually includes the experiences of the north, but rarely vice versa. Rage are the rare North American band that accepts the modernity south of the border; as a result, they've become part of that 'other us,' that 'extended us,' that Mexican youth identify with."

In an interview with the Spanish-language magazine *Re-*

forma, Zack talked about what it meant for Rage Against the Machine, or Furia Contra el Sistema, to finally play a show in Mexico. "I'm very excited, because we're finally here. I've traveled in Mexico over the last five years, and now we're finally going to play, which is something we've wanted." In the same interview Zack expressed his admiration for the courage of the Zapatista Army of National Liberation (known in Mexico as the EZLN, per the abbreviation for the army's name in Spanish) in their efforts to bring justice to the people in the beleaguered Chiapas region of Mexico. "That really remained in my heart, because I also feel Mexican. That's why I'm interested in spreading those ideas through art, because music has the power to cross borders, to break military sieges, and to establish real dialogue. Our purpose in sympathizing with the Zapatistas is to help spark that dialogue."

Given Rage's well-established revolutionary tendencies and the fact that "War within a Breath" from *The Battle of Los Angeles* directly addresses the 1994 New Year's Day rebellion by the EZLN, it's not surprising that Mexican president Ernesto Zedillo and his U.S.-endorsed Institutional Revolutionary Party (in Mexico, referred to as the PRI) wanted Rage to keep their comments from the stage to a minimum. Never shy about piping up when he smells a rat, Zack told *Spin* what the ground rules for their performance were. "The PRI said that if any artist [including Aztlan Underground and Tijuana No] commented, in any way, about the Mexican political situation, they'd be immediately expelled. Here's a party selling this democratic image to the U.S., but they want to silence anybody who criticizes them."

Following a videotaped speech by Zapatista leader Sub-commandante Marcos, addressing the problems in the Chiapas region of Mexico, Rage took the stage. The charged atmosphere in the arena, fueled by the presence of a crowd intimately acquainted with some of the injustices addressed by Rage songs, impacted the band greatly. "It was really incredible," Tom told *Addicted to Noise.* "And as were walking offstage Zack said to me, 'When people raise the finger and say, "Fuck you, I won't do what you tell me!" it resonates in a different way when you're facing some of the things that they're facing there, as opposed to what they're facing in maybe Peoria, Illinois.' But it's a healthy sentiment in Peoria, too."

Originally slated to be a benefit for the Zapatistas, Rage wound up donating the show's proceeds to victims of a recent flood in the area, at the behest of Zapatista leader Subcommandante Marcos. In an interview with the Australian radio station Triple J, Tom described the scene before the show. "Before the show there was a riot, the battle of Mexico City was being fought outside the venue. There were about six or seven thousand inside, and then there was another three and a half thousand outside who broke down the barricades to get into the show and the police riot group was called in and there was tear gas. It was pretty dramatic."

Zack's frequent volunteer work in the Chiapas region of Mexico has given him a clear picture of the people and living conditions in the area. Although NAFTA has opened up more jobs, the working conditions in the factories are well below what would be considered acceptable in the United States and the workers are paid a fraction of what U.S. workers would make. On one trip, Zack was asked to teach, so the teachers could work in the fields. In wooden classrooms with dirt floors, Zack tried his hand at teaching, in the poorest conditions imaginable. "The classroom was stuffed with forty children, all the way from kindergarden to sixth grade," Zack told *Spin*. "We taught basic math to these kids. The supplies we had were minimal; we had to break pencils several times and sharpen them so everybody had something to write with. I realized that the Mexican government had been spending hundreds of dollars a week just to keep military force in those communities, where there was nothing there kids had to write with. That shook me."

With the release date of *The Battle of Los Angeles* nearing, Rage felt relief at finally having another record, but also were glad to be finishing a work of substance. Bubblegum pop dominated 1999, with such social commentators as Britney Spears, Backstreet Boys, and 'N Sync tasting success of the multiplatinum kind. Bands that weren't of the "chew once and destroy" variety—see Korn, Limp Bizkit, and Kid Rock—all owed a weighty debt to Rage Against the Machine, influentially. In an interview with the Australian publication *The Age,* Brad said the band was eager to make an artistic contribution that came shrink-wrapped with a meaningful message inside. "Music has an incredible influence on kids in general, and right now that [fantasy] music is the flavor of the month, and we're very excited to be coming out with a record now to try to effect change in the way that we do. With a few exceptions, like the Beastie Boys, there aren't many bands being all that thoughtful. It's all about trends and kids getting caught in the whole marketing systems of record companies."

The Battle of Los Angeles came out on election day 1999 and nearly half a million fans cast their ballot for Rage and their third record in eight years. The week of its release *The Battle of Los Angeles* debuted at number one on the *Billboard* charts and sold a staggering two million records the first two months after its release. Given the bleak state of American politics, *The Battle of Los Angeles,* for some, served almost as a third-party option. Zack explained his view of the two-party system in an interview with *Vox.* "I see very little difference between the two parties. They eat from the same trough; they serve the same purpose. . . . There is very little difference between a liberal and a conservative capitalist. I have no faith, nor do I align myself with, nor do I recognize the legitimacy of the current power system."

Ironically enough, in the winter of 2000 Rage Against

the Machine became a point of contention among Republicans. In the days leading up to the frenzy of the Iowa caucus, filmmaker Michael Moore went to survey the scene, stir up some trouble, and shoot some footage for his TV show *The Awful Truth*. "We announced to all the contenders for the White House that *The Awful Truth* will endorse any candidate who jumps into our mosh pit," said Moore in an article on his official Web site. "Simple as that. No large sums of dirty money, no favors or backroom dealmaking. Just dive into the outstretched arms of a hundred degenerate — but registered — youth, and you are our candidate." George W. Bush and Steve Forbes brushed him off and Gary Bauer called the cops, but Ambassador Alan Keyes, lagging toward the back of the primary pack, took the dare and hopped in and bodysurfed to the back as Rage Against the Machine's music blared. Reactions varied: Reuters termed it "surreal"; Bauer questioned Keyes's "family values" for supporting "The Machine Rages On" (sic); and *New York Times* columnist Gail Collins pegged it as "the defining moment" of the campaign up to that point. Besides making Rage Against the Machine a well-known entity on Capitol Hill for a week or so, it underscored how far removed some political candidates are from youth culture, and made Rage's contempt for the party system all the more understandable.

Unlike *Evil Empire*, which had required a colossal collective effort to agree enough, musically and personally, to make a full record, this time out Rage emerged from the studio feeling like a stronger and more cohesive unit. "The record was really a healing process for us," Tom told Guitar.com. "I enjoyed seeing everyone and going to rehearsal and writing the songs, because from the very beginning, we felt like we were on to something here, that this would be our best work. So our mission statement was not just to make the best Rage record, but to make the best by a country mile."

With Rage, certain things can be counted on. Rage never will turn one of their songs into a fake Mentos ad. Tom and Zack will never grow long beards and hang on cars surrounded by bikini-clad women à la the facial hair–enhanced ZZ Top. You can count on the fact Rage will somehow directly expand on the lyrical (and therefore political) theme of the song. That said, just as Rage took a less obvious tack in getting their message across on *The Battle of Los Angeles,* the video for "Guerilla Radio" showcased more of the "wacky guys who play flag football" vibe that helped keep the recording process a smooth one. Designed as a parody of the Gap ads that featured similarly-clad models singing in unison, Rage's clip featured actual union members of the Garment Workers Union filling the models' inane roles. In an interview with MTV, Tom offered an understated view of the clip. "It's a takeoff on the consumerism which we've seen on some of the advertisements for certain clothing lines which have been glutting the airwaves lately."

For the filming of the "Sleep Now in the Fire" video,

Rage tapped Michael Moore, a veteran of documentary exposés such as the acclaimed film *Roger and Me*. Perhaps chosen for the delightful rabble-rousing he had created with the pit madness in Iowa, teaming Michael Moore with Rage Against the Machine meant no distracting subtleties — instead, America's most popular anti-corporate icons joined forces and aimed for America's commercial heart. Choosing to film the video on the steps of the Federal Building in New York City, across the street from the New York Stock Exchange, was bound to make headlines one way or another; the only question on that January day in the year 2000 was which direction it would come from. In an interview with MTV, Moore explained their choice. "We decided to shoot this video in the belly of the beast." Rage set up their gear in front of the Stock Exchange and ran through "Sleep Now in the Fire" six times. After the sixth time, the cops arrived on the scene. In a posting on his official Web site — www.michaelmoore.com — Moore talked about how the mayhem they knew was coming, ultimately took shape. "They ordered the makeshift concert to cease, but before we had a chance to stop, four officers jumped me and put me in one of those police locks like you see on that excellent and informative show *COPS*. One tried to break my arm, the other put a chokehold on my neck. In all my years of shooting in New York, I have never had this happen, and all I could think of was, well, I just hope it's a new plunger."

According to Moore's description of events, the crowd

then hopped police barricades and made a beeline for the double doors of the New York Stock Exchange. But before the band and the horde of fans sprinting along with them could get there, a set of large steel gates slammed down in front of the next set of double doors and the NYSE closed an hour early, for the first time that most anyone could recall. In an interview with the *Socialist Worker*, Tom offered a similar account. "We invited Rage Against the Machine fans to come along and join us in our video. Around three hundred showed up. Suddenly the police arrived and arrested Michael. They dragged him off to jail. The rest of us stormed the Stock Exchange. About two hundred of us got through the first set of doors, but our charge was stopped when the Stock Exchange's titanium riot doors came crashing down. Our protest stopped trading at the Stock Exchange for the last two hours of the day."

For Moore's part he was arrested, but the band and their fans managed to avoid getting hauled downtown. It sounded like the stuff that press releases are made of. The clever folks at Epic who are charged with promoting the records Rage makes couldn't have drummed up a better stunt if they tried: the anti-capitalist band playing the capitalist media like a fiddle. Rage may not like the machine but they certainly know what makes it run.

With their sporadic recording pattern, the live show is where all the bottled-up energy pours on out. And while Rage prides itself on an unparalleled ability to ignite an arena-sized crowd, Tim noted with surprise before the band embarked on the *Battle of Los Angeles* tour that they haven't played all that much. "I can't remember the exact number, but it was like 380 shows. I was thinking we'd played more like a thousand," Tim told *Rolling Stone*. "We take the time, and it builds up the angst. Then when we go onstage, it's not all 'Hey!'—big smile on face, rockin' with the girls. It's fierce rock always."

The tour opened in Oakland with banners proclaiming "The Battle of Oakland" sailing high above the stage. In a review that ran on Rollingstone.com, Greg Heller praised the aptness of the battle metaphor and said Rage's combative opening-night effort went a long way toward winning the opening skirmish of a twenty-date way. "If the sonic offensive launched in Oakland is any indication, the analogy of Rage show as combat will work in every city they power through. This tour, it seems, means war. So when singer/rapper Zack de la Rocha leapt up and kicked in the gig, asking the packed house, 'Who controls the present now?' in 'Testify,' he became the incendiary general, prepping his Bay Area troops for a night in the trenches."

Using the same logic that compelled them to sign with a major label, Rage made a beeline for the hit factory responsible for turning, Christina, and Mandy into household names, and made 'N Sync and Backstreet Boys the biggest thing this side of the New Kids on the Block when it came time to promote an album. MTV's *Total Request*

Live (known as *TRL* to the hip eight-year-olds that com-
prise its audience) hosted by Carson Daly, features incom-
plete clips of videos, hysterical fans, and occasionally
bands. Tom discussed Rage's reasoning for appearing on
the mindless program. "I never want to be elitist, and that's
where a lot of kids see their music. We weren't going to
skip the show because Britney Spears rather than Soundgarden may be on the day after us. The only concern for
us is that the music and the politics are uncut. It's not like
we are donning midriff outfits and sweaters in order to
pander to the programmers or the audience. . . . There was
a raging debate on some of the Web sites. Some fans didn't
like us going on there, but, again, I think there's nothing
better than having our video for 'Guerrilla Radio' in between a couple of those whack-ass videos that they're playing these days."

The Fraternal Order of Police, still bitter at Rage for
pulling off the Mumia Abu-Jamal benefit over the FOP's
vociferous objections, made a bid to slow the promotion
of *The Battle of Los Angeles.* Concerned that Rage was
being given a chance to spread their message on the national forum provided by the *Late Night with Conan
O'Brien* show, the Fraternal Order of Police drafted a letter
to Bob Wright, president and CEO of NBC, requesting
that the network not air the show, or at least omit Rage's
performance. In the letter, the FOP went so far as to suggest that Mumia was profiting from killing a police officer,

when in fact the money raised from the benefit concert went to his legal fund, an entity that would not be necessary if he was not on death row under some questionable circumstances surrounding his conviction.

Erik Whittington, director of Rock for Life, an anti–abortion rights organization, took his shots at the band also, terming them "baby killers" and attempting to link Rage to communism, Nazis, and the murders at Columbine High School in Colorado with one sloppy sweep. "Because music fans continue to buy Rage Against the Machine CDs and concert tickets, the band is given a huge platform to spew their hateful propaganda while thousands numbfully accept it as gospel. Marx is the author of the most oppressive political regimes in history, Lenin starved millions of his own people, and Nietzsche's philosophy justified the Nazi regime. Is this the kind of band parents want their children listening to? Is it any wonder why tragedies such as the one at Columbine High School take place? We've had enough of violence, hate, and death. Turn Rage Against the Machine off. Tell radio DJs not to play their music, don't buy their CDs, and tell everyone you know to do the same."

Having been through this boycott routine before, Tim offered the verbal equivalent of a shrug in an interview with Launch.com, at the news that Rage were now enemies of Rock for Life. "There's always going to be those people who don't agree with what we're talking about. And if they want to spend the time and energy, ultimately they just help us out. So I'd like to thank these people for fucking selling [our] records, which is what they're going to do by doing this."

Given the fact that Rage released *The Battle of Los Angeles* on election day 1999, it's probably not surprising that when the Democratic National Convention came to Los Angeles, Rage decided to play a free show as part of a protest against the United States' rigid two-party system. One of the greatest controversies of what at the time was the bland election of 2000 was the fact that third-party candidates such as Ralph Nader of the Green Party and Pat Buchanan of the Reform Party were barred from the national debates between Democratic nominee Vice President Al Gore and the Republican candidate, George W. Bush. Concerned that the agendas of the two candidates were too closely linked to those of the multinational corporations that fund much of the campaigns, Rage and the multiethnic L.A. band Ozomatli agreed to play in a fenced-in area within one hundred yards of the Staples Center, where Al Gore was inside addressing the Democrats and planting that famous smooch on Tipper's mug. Big-screen TVs beamed the action from inside the Staples Center to the eight thousand or so fans who had come to see Rage play. Once Rage launched into "Bulls on Parade," all attention was focused on the front. By playing the convention, Rage were following in the footsteps of the political Detroit band the MC5, who had played outside the infamous 1968 Democratic National Convention in Chicago.

In a nod to the MC5's gig at that riot-plagued convention, Rage treated the crowd on hand to their update of the MC5's anthem, "Kick Out the Jams." Strangely though, Zack refrained from making almost any political commentary other than, "Brothers and sisters, our democracy has been hijacked" — which coming from him is roughly equivalent to casual party conversation. Riots broke out after Ozomatli's set was curtailed by the Los Angeles police, who had deemed the increasingly hostile crowd's actions sufficient to make the gathering an unlawful assembly, but by that time Rage had long since been whisked away.

In the summer of 2000, Rage announced a thirty-date North American tour with the Beastie Boys; titled Rhyme and Reason 2000, the tour paired up a couple of bands known for their extensive activist work. Not surprisingly, soon after the announcement came the news that the bands would donate one dollar of each ticket sold to charities of their choice, with the Beastie Boys favoring the Tibet-affiliated Milarepa Fund and Rage splitting their portion among a variety of non-profits. The two acts picked a rotating array of openers that reflected the diversity both bands favor in their own music, with Busta Rhymes, No Doubt, Common, At the Drive-In, and Mos Def among those who got the nod to hop on board. On the phone from Japan where Rage were playing their first Japanese shows in support of *The Battle of Los Angeles*, Tom talked to MTV about teaming up with the Beastie Boys. "We're played some shows in the past, some benefit shows, together. It was an idea that was long overdue. I mean the idea is a very simple one. It's time to make the funkiest, most rocking, greatest tour of all time. Beastie Boys, Rage. You've got your conscious music and your shockingly fat jams colliding right and left and we can't wait."

The highly anticipated tour was at first delayed after Mike D from the Beastie Boys hit a pothole on his bike and dislocated his shoulder. Initially the tour was pushed back and then finally scrapped with little explanation given, beyond the standard "scheduling conflicts." In an interview with *SonicNet*, Tom offered a reply that seemed to point a finger at Zack and at the same time suggested that again Rage might be having the kind of problems that once had threatened their future as a band.

"I'd do it today, Tom told *SonicNet*. "We just don't have a consensus among all seven bandmembers [between the two bands] to make it happen right now. . . . The Beastie Boys are ready to go, and Timmy, Brad, and I are ready to go. We're just not all ready to go."

With the Rhyme and Reason tour scrapped and Rage getting shut out at the MTV Music Awards in New York City, it took Tim rocking the boat . . . er, prop . . . for Rage to make headlines. Cementing his reputation as the wild card of the band, Tim protested Limp Bizkit's win in the Best Rock Video category of the MTV awards show by climbing a prop shaped like the Statue of Liberty, swaying back and forth at the top of it, and screaming. Limp Bizkit were oblivious to his presence for the most part and when they did notice the commotion, singer Fred Durst failed to recognize Tim and urged him to make the twenty-plus–foot jump to the ground. Security removed Tim and delivered him into the waiting arms of the NYPD, who gave him a one-night iron vacation before releasing him early the next day. No one was more surprised than Tim's bandmates. In an interview with Rollingstone.com both Tom and Zack expressed disappointment in his actions. "I had no idea what he was planning," Tom said. "I didn't expect an evening of Tim versus the NYPD. Earlier, Tim had mentioned something about toppling the podium if we won, for no particular reason, which seemed silly to me. Right before the award we were up for was announced, Tim asked Zack and me if he should do it. We both said no." For his part Zack sounded appalled, telling Rollingstone.com, "I was so humiliated. I left"—and added that he would be taking a long walk to think about the situation.

Less than a week later Rage was back in Los Angeles at the Olympic Grand Auditorium to record a live album. Originally the band had planned to record the live album in San Francisco and booked three nights at the historic Fillmore, but after twice canceling scheduled dates they decided to stay in Los Angeles and play at the former boxing arena. Despite the ubiquitous presence of video cameras and mikes, on the first night Zack said nothing from the stage that the *Rock Star Manual* says singers are supposed to say about recording live albums and, in fact, he gave no indication that this show was any different from their others. The evening's set was split between Rage standards such as "Bulls on Parade," "Killing in the Name," and "Testify," and covers including the MC5's "Kick Out the Jams," Cypress Hill's "How I Could Just Kill a Man," EPMD's "I'm Housin'," and Eric B. and Rakim's "Microphone Fiend."

In an interview with *CDNow* Tom explained Rage's decision to record a live album at this particular juncture of their career. "The one thing that we do best is we play live. Throughout our career we haven't yet documented that in the way that I think that we can make the definitive Rage Against the Machine record as a live record. This is the new Rage record; every time we go out, we go out to make the best Rage record, and we're taking that very seriously this time. In the last decade or so most live albums have been kind of throwaways to meet some record-company year-end numbers, and we definitely didn't want to do that. We wanted to make a definitive Rage record like the Who's *Live at Leeds* or something like that, where you distill the essence of the band into a live recording."

To accompany the live album Rage recorded a slew of covers with producer Rick Rubin, songs that greatly stretched the boundaries of what a Rage Against the Machine song should sound like. "I hate to call them covers, but we take the lyrics from other songs and write brand new Rage Against the Machine tracks underneath," Tom told *SonicNet*. "Dylan's 'Maggie's Farm' sounds maybe more like a Black Sabbath song than a Bob Dylan song, and Devo's 'Beautiful World' sounds more like a Woody Guthrie campfire ballad than new wave. It's really one of the most liberating and exciting creative experiences I've ever been involved in. Even with Rage Against the Machine, there are precious few rules, but with this, we've completely thrown out any conventions." Other covers recorded in the sessions included Minor Threat's "In My Eyes," Cypress Hill's "How I Could Just Kill a Man," and the Rolling Stones' "Street Fighting Man."

If the year 2000 taught Rage fans anything it's that nearly a decade into it, Rage is calm like a bomb. Plans change on a moment's notice and one misstep could easily upset the delicate chemistry that has thus far held them together. In chat rooms the buzz is nearly audible as fans try to put the pieces together. Canceled shows, embarrassed band members, arrests, compelling new side projects—any one of these might become the hiccup in the line that sends the four members of Rage going their separate ways. If and when Rage split and their publicist sends out the inevitable press release assuring that the band is parting on "amicable terms" and that the breakup is due to "personal differences," there won't be any new music from Rage, but in an interview with *CDNow* Tom suggested that Rage's lasting impact will likely be judged by factors other than the number of songs they wrote or the number of records sold.

"It's not enough for us to dabble in feel-good issues and

do the occasional benefit show, but [instead we really try] to build a bridge between our pretty sizable audience and the world of getting-your-hands-dirty activism. And the band's success, in the end, I think, will be judged not by record sales, but by tangible gains in the world."

EPILOGUE

So the bubble burst. The tension that had boiled just under the surface spilled over. The egos swelled, heads got cloudy, and the juggernaut derailed. This was the one they couldn't work through. Just a day after St. Martin's received a glistening copy of the final edits for this book, the end came in the form of a terse and awkwardly-worded press release from Zack.

"I feel that it is now necessary to leave Rage because our decision-making process has completely failed. It is no longer meeting the aspirations of all four of us collectively as a band, and from my perspective, has undermined our artistic and political ideal. I am extremely proud of our work, both as activists and musicians, as well as indebted and grateful to every person who has expressed solidarity and shared this incredible experience with us."

Tom echoed the essence of Zack's statement in an interview on MTV. "The decision-making process has broken down for everyone. I have no hard feelings, and we wish Zack well with his project. But everyone is excited about the twenty-nine live and cover tracks that we have in the can, and some of it will be released in the fall."

And just like that, it was over. Rage's label, Epic Records, made a tentative plan to release the album of covers recorded with Rick Rubin in December 2000, with the live album to follow in 2001. Not talked about but certainly planned was the inevitable greatest-hits album and producers at VH-1's *Behind the Music* were reported to have been seen gleefully rubbing their hands together and placing informational calls.

The next day brought a counterstatement from the three remaining members of Rage, saying, "We are committed to continuing with our efforts to effect change in the social and political arena and look forward to creating more groundbreaking music for our fans," the band said in a press release. "In other words, we'll keep it loud, keep it funky and most definitely rock on. We're proud of our history and what we've accomplished musically and politically over the last nine years."

The day after that, director Michael Moore, the guy who'd told the gaffers and the key grips what to do on the last few Rage videos, weighed in with his opinion. "I know the three of them felt strongly about going on this tour, but Zack felt strongly about wanting to do this solo album that he was putting off," Moore told *SonicNet*. "He decided he'd put off his album long enough, and he wanted to do it. They all respect each other greatly and care for each other. Frankly, I take Zack at his word, but I wouldn't rule out the possibility of seeing these guys back together again."

Final or not, the fact Rage had played their last, struck a chord with fans and performers and the obits poured in. Coby Dick, frontman of Papa Roach—so named for being one of the unkillable bands who cluttered the path behind Rage—paid his respects on *MTV News.* "That band was like the grandfather of a style, of this whole rap-rock music. Why do the good bands have to break up?" lamented Dick. "Either somebody dies, or they break up. I think that their music will go down in history, and I think that Rage Against the Machine really left their mark. The only thing I wish is that we could have played with them."

Buoyed by the news that Tim, Tom, and Brad were intent on keeping the faith, chat rooms buzzed with suggestions for potential new frontmen, ranging from the absurd Sammy Hagar end of the spectrum, to the what-if of rappers like KRS-One and Chuck D.

In an interview with Chuck D the week after Rage split up, the Public Enemy frontman offered a philosophical take on the breakup. "I talked to Tom Morello yesterday. Things happen with groups sometimes. It's unfortunate given the following and meaning that Rage has had that this has come to pass at this point. Zack wanted an artistic outlet and he felt he was on a treadmill. It's hard to get four people to go one straight way for that long. They already had done it for nine years in a row; I think Zack wanted to escape for a second."

In the background fellow Public Enemy rapper Professor Griff chimed in. "Can I say something, can I just say one thing? When I first heard Rage broke up I called a couple people and I went on the Internet to see if they'd really broken up. My reaction was, the revolution has been interrupted, they were the voice that carried this thing."

As for the popular rumor that Chuck D would step into Zack's sizable shoes, the rapper dismissed it out of hand. "No, I'm forty-years-old. I'm not considering being the leader of any group. I've got too much respect. I guess if it was fifteen years ago and it was a Sammy Hagar–type thing then maybe, but no, it's out of the question. . . . Anybody that replaces Zack right now, it's not going to be Rage, it's going to be something else."

Fugees mastermind Wyclef Jean threw his hat into the narrow political rock arena on his solo album *Ecleftic* with the track "Diallo"—a tribute to Amadou Diallo, who was shot at forty-one times in the vestibule of his own apartment building, by four New York City police officers, while reaching for his wallet. In an interview soon after Rage parted ways, Wyclef said what millions of fans already knew. "Rage is one of my favorite groups. They did stand for something. Now I don't know what's going on. No one stands for nothing anymore. It's sad. I think they were one of a kind."

*   *   *

RAGE AGAINST THE MACHINE

As the interminable editing process for this book slogged on, more and more information about Rage in the post-bust-up era leaked out. That covers album recorded with Rick Rubin became *Renegades* and sold a copious amount of copies.

In subsequent interviews band members sounded increasingly philosophical about the split. Talking to *Rolling Stone*, Tim basically said he saw it coming. "There's always been this looming solo record thing—Zack was vocal about what he wanted to do for a long time. It's hard for me to get bummed out about it. I'm looking back on ten years, thinking that was a great thing. But there is a lot more to be accomplished."

Tim, Tom, and Brad spent the months after Zack left searching for singers. After the initial flurry of rumors it was confirmed that former Soundgarden singer Chris Cornell was in rehearsals with the trio of remaining members.

At the 2001 Grammys—where, oh yeah, Rage picked up another Grammy for the Best Hard Rock Performance—Tom Morello raved about working with Cornell. "He's one of the greatest singers and songwriters in rock history, and jamming with him was off the hook," Morello told *SonicNet*. "We were just making up new, exciting rock. . . . Chris Cornell is definitely not the singer of Rage Against the Machine, but the music that we made in the couple of days that we jammed together was really groundbreaking and fantastic, and was so exciting. He's amazing."

On the day St. Martin's hired thug came beating down

the door in search of the final second pass pages, or some silly publishing demand in that vein, some reports even had Cornell joining the band, but under a new group name.

For his part, Zack broke his long-standing post-breakup silence with an interview in *Spin*. Not surprisingly, for Zack the band breakup stemmed from his age-old disagreement with Tom over the direction the band should go in. "Every time we entered a studio, this arm wrestling match would start between what I heard, which was more of an Afrika Bambaataa meets Sonic Youth type of thing, and what Tom heard, which was Jimmy Page and Tony Iommi," Zack said to *Spin*. "It rarely extended past those boundaries, and that slow evolution was one of the reasons I became so exhausted. Toward the end, it was clear that there were no musical risks being taken. You could basically tell what a Rage record was going to sound like before you even heard it."

Zack spoke glowingly of his collaborations with DJ Shadow, terming the experience "refreshing," and looked forward to working with Ahmir from the Roots and El-P, formerly of Company Flow.

What no one talked about was getting the band back together.